Outspoken. Original. Provocative.

index
on censorship

Margaret Atwood Isaac
Babel **Daniel Barenboim**
Samuel Beckett Mikhail
Bulgakov William Boyd
Noam Chomsky Ariel
Dorfman **Shirin Ebadi**
Umberto **Eco** Harold
Evans Nadine Gordimer

The world's best
authors, artists and
thinkers write for
Index on Censorship

Milan Kundera Osip Ma
Colin Greenwood Václav
Christopher Hitchens Arth
Salman Rushdie Will Self A
Soyinka Tom Stoppard A
Ugresic Mario Vargas Llos

As the world's most influential free expression magazine, Index on Censorship is a must read for free thinkers everywhere. For 40 years, it has reported on free expression violations, published banned writing and given a voice to those who have been prevented from speaking out.

From freedom of information and state control of the internet to whistleblowing and jokes on Twitter, free expression is one of today's most challenging issues and something that affects us all. Through challenging and intelligent analysis, Index on Censorship sets the agenda for the most urgent free expression issues of the day.

delstam Adam Michnik
Havel Bernard-Henri Lévy
Miller Anna Politkovskaya
exander Solzhenitsyn Wole
ng San Suu Kyi Dubravka
Kurt Vonnegut Ai Weiwei

Save 40%

To celebrate the 40th anniversary of Index on Censorship, we're offering 40% off print subscriptions to Volume 41. This includes our special anniversary issue, which features an exclusive essay by Aung San Suu Kyi, the first publication of an extract from Ariel Dorfman's new play, Magnum photographer Abbas's photo essay on free speech in Iran and an interview with Flemming Rose, the journalist who commissioned the Danish cartoons. We're also making our remarkable literary archive available so you can read some of the ground-breaking articles from the last 40 years.

For more information, go to:
www.indexoncensorship.org/magazine-archive

How to subscribe

Index on Censorship is published four times a year by SAGE. It is available in print, online and through the Index app.

To enjoy 40% off individual print subscriptions to Volume 41, contact SAGE Customer Services, quoting 40YIOCBR1*.
Email: subscriptions@sagepub.co.uk
Tel: +44 (0) 20 7324 8701

For online subscriptions, go to **indexoncensorship.org/magazine**
For the Index on Censorship app, go to iTunes.com

*Offer applies to Volume 41 only. After 2012, your subscription will revert to the full price.

Index on Censorship

Free Word Centre, 60 Farringdon Road, London, ECIR 3GA

Chief Executive John Kampfner **Deputy Chief Executive** Rohan Jayasekera **Editor** Jo Glanville **Finance Manager** David Sewell **Head of Events** Sara Rhodes **Online Editor** Emily Butselaar **News Editor** Padraig Reidy **Assistant Editor** Natasha Schmidt **Head of Advocacy** Michael Harris **Head of Development** Lizzie Rusbridger **Head of Communications** Pam Cowburn **Programme Manager, Arts** Julia Farrington **Events Assistant** Eve Jackson **Editorial Assistants** Marta Cooper, Alice Purkiss, Sara Yasin **Research Assistant** Carlette Jannink **Events Coordinator** Tamara Micner
Graphic designer Sam Hails
Cover design www.byboth.com
Printed by Page Bros., Norwich, UK

Volume 41 No 1 2012

If you are interested in republishing any article featured in this issue, please contact us at permissions@indexoncensorship.org

Supported by
ARTS COUNCIL ENGLAND

Vol 12 No 3 June 1983

Vol 13 No 6 December 1984

INDEX on

INDEX on
CENSORSHIP

Vol 11 No 1 February 1982 £1.85 $3.95

POLAND

INDEX on
CENSORSHIP

Vol 12 No 1 February 1983

Playing for the people **Miguel Angel Estrella**
'Subversive' music in Chile **ILLAPU**
China: the difficulty of walking on two legs **David Holm**
Plastic People of Czechoslovakia **Ivan Jirous, Vratislav Brabene**
Hans Werner Henze and Hanns Eisler **Paul Hamburger**
Protecting Soviet music from dangerous ideas **Michael Goldstein**
Kenya's banned musical **Ngugi wa Thiong'o**
Musicians under apartheid **Barry Gilder**
Israel, Wagner and Strauss **Nancy Uscher**
Convenient illusions **Michael Tippett**

MUSIC IS
DANGEROUS

Catch 28
s: Lying in
o touch th
cendiary be
& the med
ka, Bangla

NYA
ui: Cry fo
bdalla: M
of a univ
of repre

THE PRACTICE OF FREEDOM

Jo Glanville

A few years after the fall of the Berlin Wall, one of *Index*'s funders informed the magazine's staff that it was time to pull down the shutters and go home: job done, censorship was now a thing of the past. The anecdote is highly revealing of a certain misguided attitude towards censorship – namely, that it is a creature purely of totalitarianism, and communist totalitarianism at that. Although Cold War dissidents, from Solzhenitsyn to Václav Havel, featured significantly from the very first appearance of *Index* 40 years ago in the spring of 1972, when the magazine was founded in response to an appeal for help from the Soviet Union, *Index* made it clear from the start that censorship was a worldwide issue that featured in democracies as well as in dictatorships. 'The problem of censorship is part of larger ones about the use and abuse of freedom,' wrote the poet Sir Stephen Spender in the first issue.

It was Spender who founded the organisation Writers and Scholars International (WSI), the parent body of *Index*, to support freedom of expression. He had been moved by a letter published in *The Times* by the Russian dissident Pavel Litvinov, grandson of Stalin's foreign minister, who had bravely made a stand. Spender brought together the greatest writers, artists and intellectuals of the day to send their support, including W H Auden and Henry Moore. He then enlisted David Astor, editor of the *Observer*, the biographer Elizabeth Longford and the lawyer Louis Blom-Cooper, amongst others, to join WSI's council. It was the idea of Russia specialist Michael Scammell, *Index*'s first editor, to start a magazine.

Looking back through *Index*'s archive has been a revelation. It is not simply the roll-call of the greatest names in international literature (Nadine Gordimer, Mario Vargas Llosa, Samuel Beckett, Kurt Vonnegut), it is also the unchanging texture of censorship and totalitarianism, whatever the technology. There seems to be very little difference between the tactics of the NKVD, Stalin's secret police, in 1939 and the Chinese police today.

In 1991, *Index* published, for the first time in English, a remarkable series of documents from the Lubianka, the KGB headquarters. This includes the devastating record of the interrogation of the celebrated Russian-Jewish writer Isaac Babel, murdered by Stalin's regime in 1940. In a forced confession in 1939, Babel is reported as saying: 'I wrote contrary to the interest of the masses and the Party, I fell into slanderous generalisations concerning the situation in the country and attacked the current leadership.' Compare this with the imprisonment of the Chinese dissident Chen Wei last December, for 'inciting subversion of state power'. There is no greater crime than challenging, or being perceived to challenge, the one-party state.

Chen Wei was a signatory of Charter 08, a manifesto for reform co-written by Nobel Peace Prize winner Liu Xiaobo. The Charter is modelled on the famous Czech document Charter 77 and Václav Havel, one of its architects and a regular contributor to *Index* in the 70s and 80s, remains an inspiration for Chinese dissidents. You can read one of Chen Wei's powerful essays which led to his trial in this issue on pp. 107–113, and you can find Václav Havel's essays and the interrogation of Isaac Babel in our archive. In celebration of *Index*'s anniversary, our publisher SAGE is generously making the archive of the magazine freely available online from 26 March until the end of the year. You can access the archive at http://www.indexoncensorship.org/magazine-archive. It is a literary treasure trove and also an historic document of the extremes of human behaviour – from man at his most inhumane to his most courageous.

What's clear is that censorship never dies, it simply changes its form. Technology can provide a route around it, but will never put the censors out of action. It is still up to the dissidents, the protesters, the whistleblowers, the artists and the writers to get the word out through their sheer determination. As Aung San Suu Kyi, one of the most remarkable freedom fighters of our time, writes in this issue: 'When we write about our right to freedom of expression we begin to practice it. There can be no theoretical advocacy of these freedoms, there can only be practical, practising advocacy.'

Take advantage of our special anniversary discount offer of 40 per cent on an annual subscription by calling SAGE Customer Services on +44 (0) 207 324 8701, quoting 40YIOCM1. *Index on Censorship* has now grown into an organisation that fights for freedom of expression around the world. You can support our projects and follow the latest censorship stories around the world at www.indexoncensorship.org ❐

©Jo Glanville
41(1): 3/5
DOI: 10.1177/0306422012440062
www.indexoncensorship.org

CONTENTS

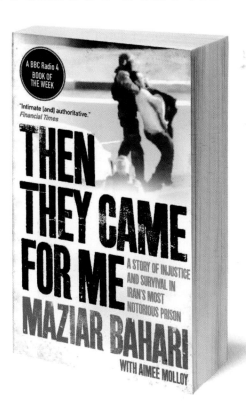

GRIT IN THE ENGINE

Robert McCrum considers *Index*'s role in the history of the fight for free speech, from the oppression of the Cold War to censorship online

In February 1663, the London printer John Twyn waited in Newgate prison for his execution, the unique horror of being hanged, drawn and quartered at Tyburn, the place known today as Marble Arch. This medieval agony was the recently restored monarch King Charles II's terrifying lesson to his subjects: do not write, or print, treason against the state.

Even more cruel, Twyn's offence was merely to have printed an anonymous pamphlet justifying the people's right to rebellion, 'mettlesome stuff' according to the state censor (the King's Surveyor of the Press). No one suggested that Twyn had written this treason, only that he had transformed it from manuscript to print. Perhaps he hadn't even read it. Never mind: he was sentenced to death.

Pressed both to admit his offence and reveal the name of the pamphlet's anonymous author (and thereby save his own life), Twyn refused. In words of breathtaking courage that echo down the centuries, he told the prison chaplain that 'it was not his principle to betray the Author'. Shortly afterwards, Twyn went to his doom. His head was placed on a spike over Ludgate, and his dismembered body distributed round other city gates.

Words can be weapons, and the pen challenges the sword. Writers, and printers, 'the troublers of the poor world's peace', in Shakespeare's phrase, have always seemed a danger to the state. Across Europe, for the first three centuries of the printing press, questions of religion and politics were usually settled by the authorities of the day with rare and explicit savagery. As John Mullan has shown in his excellent monograph *Anonymity*, the safest course for the dissident writer was a pseudonymous or anonymous cloak of identity.

Eventually, the Romantic assertion of the heroic individual's place in the world at the beginning of the 19th century ended this prudent convention, but slowly. The scandalous first two Cantos of *Don Juan* were printed without naming either Lord Byron or his publisher, John Murray. Despite the risks, the poet soon found fame irresistible. 'Own that I am the author,' he instructed Murray, 'I will never shrink.' By the reign of the fourth George, Britain's liberal democracy was never likely to eviscerate, hang or decapitate a transgressive writer, though some terrible penalties did remain on the statute book for decades to come.

Abroad in Europe, as repressive states, notably Tsarist Russia, grew harsher, the fate of writers worsened, but hardly varied. The essential predicament was unchanged from John Twyn's day. Putting black on white, words on the page, as accurately and truthfully as one could, would never fail to make trouble with vested interests, arterio-sclerotic authorities and evil despotisms. Dostoevsky was marched before a firing squad, but reprieved. The distinguished list of writers, before the Cold War, who died for their art includes Osip Mandelstam and Isaac Babel, possibly the greatest loss of all.

By the middle of the 20th century there was, in the words of Graham Greene, a fairly general recognition that 'it had always been in the interests of the State to poison the psychological wells, to encourage cat-calls, to restrict human sympathy. It makes government easier when people shout Gallilean, Papist, Fascist, Communist.' In the same essay, on 'the virtues of disloyalty', Greene expressed the writer's credo in an age of growing state control. 'The writer is driven by his own vocation,' he said, 'to be a Protestant in a Catholic society, a Catholic in a Protestant one, to see the virtues of the Capitalist in a Communist society, of the Communist in a Capitalist state.' Greene concludes this celebration of opposition by quoting Tom Paine: 'We must guard even our enemies against injustice.'

Confronted by the intractable collision of the creative individual of fiery conscience with the frozen monolith of the powers that be, there is one essential question: What Is to Be Done? In 1968, the poet Stephen Spender, sickened and dismayed by reports of literary repression in Russia,

Czechoslovakia, Greece, Spain, Portugal, Brazil and South Africa (as well as several recently decolonised African states), responded to the spirit of a revolutionary year. He decided to organise a fight-back, setting the pen against the sword, based in London.

George Orwell had already pointed out, in his 1946 essay 'The Prevention of Literature', that 'literature has sometimes flourished under despotic regimes, but the despotisms of the past were not totalitarian'. In fact, it was the totalitarian regime of the USSR, and its trial of Yuli Daniel and Andrei Sinyavsky, that proved the tipping-point for Spender. He was joined by Pavel Litvinov, the Soviet scientist, dissident and human rights activist, who wrote an open letter asking if it might not be possible to form in England an organisation of intellectuals who would make it their business to publish information about what was happening to their censored, suppressed and imprisoned colleagues abroad. Litvinov was inspired by the fates of fellow Russians, but he insisted that such an organisation should operate internationally and not just concern itself with victims of Soviet oppression, though their plight was possibly the worst in those dark days of the Cold War.

Spender, who was exceedingly well-connected, organised a telegram of support in response to Litvinov's appeal, signed by an awesome roll-call of the great: Cecil Day-Lewis, Yehudi Menuhin, WH Auden, Henry Moore, AJ Ayer, Bertrand Russell, Julian Huxley, Mary McCarthy, JB Priestley and his wife Jacquetta Hawkes, Paul Scofield, Igor Stravinsky, Stuart Hampshire, Maurice Bowra and George Orwell's widow, Sonia. These, and subsequently many others, declared they would 'help in any way possible'.

This initiative led, in turn, to the formation of the Council of WSI (Writers and Scholars International), whose founding members included David Astor, editor of the *Observer*, Elizabeth Longford, Roland Penrose, Louis Blom-Cooper and Spender himself. *Index on Censorship* was born when Michael Scammell, an expert on Russia, came up with the idea of founding a magazine. Thus was the ongoing battle for 'intellectual freedom' moved onto new terrain best suited

1974 – Soviet Union

Author Alexander Solzhenitsyn is expelled and charged with treason following the publication of *The Gulag Archipelago*, which documents life in the country's labour camps. Solzhenitsyn had already spent eight years in prison for his writing.

If Samuel Beckett had been born in Czechoslovakia we'd still be Waiting for Godot.

Samuel Beckett's "Waiting for Godot" is banned in Czechoslovakia. In fact, any writing that differs from the opinions of the Czech government is banned in Czechoslovakia.

Luckily, Beckett does not live in Czechoslovakia, but what of those writers who do?

Fortunately, some of their work can be read in Censorship, a to writers and scholars – the printed word published in a little magazine. Soon, the advantages and benefits of fighting oppression from a dedicated bastion of free expression became obvious to both sides, free and unfree alike.

Index, whose first issue appeared in 1972, declared that its aim was to 'record and analyse all forms of inroads into freedom of expression'. Further, it would 'examine the censorship situation in individual countries' and would publish 'censored material in the journal'. In the long and bloody history of the fight for intellectual freedom there had been many impassioned statements of principle about the writer's role as a piece of grit in the engine of the state. No one, however, had ever thought to jam a whole toolbox into the machinery of power, and place a fully-funded institution (such as WSI) in direct opposition to the repressive intentions of despotic regimes. This was the unique and historic importance of *Index*. But its success was not a foregone conclusion. Spender, its founder, was fully alert to the potential for windbaggery and failure inherent in such a venture. There was, he wrote, 'the risk that the magazine will become simply a bulletin of frustration'.

Actually, the opposite came to pass. *Index* became a clarion voice in the cause of free expression. The abuses of freedom worldwide in the 1970s were so appalling and so widespread that the magazine rapidly found itself in the frontline of campaigns against repression and censorship in Russia, Czechoslovakia, Latin America and South Africa. Alongside Amnesty International and the PEN Club, *Index* gave vivid expression to the truth that 'censorship' today takes many cruel forms: writers who are sent to labour camps, or blackmailed by threats to their families, or harassed into silence and isolation.

Perhaps the most important thing *Index* did, from the beginning, was to universalise an issue that was in peril of becoming a special interest: freedom was not 'a luxury enjoyed by bourgeois individualists'. Along with self-expression, it was a human right, and an instrument of human consciousness that should be fought for worldwide.

1977 – Czechoslovakia

Charter 77 (Charta 77), an informal civil initiative promoting freedom of opinion and expression, is drafted. Signatories include Czech playwright Václav Havel. The document becomes a template for future campaigns to support free speech around the world.

Historically, the classic polemical statement against censorship, John Milton's *Areopagitica*, a pamphlet against the Licensing Order of 1643, had focused on the English Parliament's threat to a free press. Milton, writing in the midst of Civil War, was less worried about blood than ink: 'Who kills a man kills a reasonable creature, God's image,' he writes, 'but he who destroys a good book, kills reason itself.' Three centuries later, *Index* would concern itself with both the breath of the oppressed writer but also the life-blood of liberty, namely, free expression.

In an astonishingly short time, barely a generation, from 1972 to 1989, the magazine established itself as a force to be reckoned with. At first, it took up the issue that had inspired its beginnings: Soviet oppression. In defence of Alexander Solzhenitsyn, *Index* published part of a long, autobiographical poem, 'God Keep Me from Going Mad', composed in 1950-53 while Solzhenitsyn was serving a sentence in a labour camp in North Kazakhstan, the setting for *One Day in the Life of Ivan Denisovich*. This was followed by a scoop in 1973, the unexpurgated text of an interview Solzhenitsyn had given to AP and *Le Monde* in which the writer revealed that 'preparations are being made to have me killed in a motor accident'.

The importance of this document, one of the writer's very rare accounts of his predicament, is that it described in horrifying and particular detail the true nature of the Soviet regime's campaign against him, especially the constant surveillance and the unrelenting menace of the state's agents. Solzhenitsyn was also able to draw attention to the persecution of Andrei Sakharov. In the bleakest depths of the Cold War, taking up the cause of Russia's dissident community made the difference between international recognition and utter oblivion.

As the magazine grew in confidence, it began to focus on other, related injustices behind the Iron Curtain, notably in Czechoslovakia (as it was). It was among the first to publish the banned playwright Václav Havel in English. In 1976, a retrospective on Czechoslovakia eight years after the Soviet invasion of Prague described how Havel was being 'constantly harassed and persecuted by the authorities', the beginning (as it turned out) of a long assault on Havel's liberty.

When Charter 77 was formed the following year, *Index* became a vital link in the chain of communication between the *samizdat* literary community in Prague and the wider world. The exiled Czech journalist George Theiner, who succeeded Michael Scammell as editor, strengthened this link. Context and continuity, the steady accumulation of a body of work and opinion, are vital ingredients in any effective campaign on behalf of oppressed writers. *Index* now provided both a sober and authoritative framework for its protest and

also, through the office in London, a team of journalists dedicated to monitoring the devious and sinister machinations of oppressive regimes worldwide.

In the 1980s, the magazine spread its wings. There were exposés of repression in Latin America and persecution in Africa (Kenya, Nigeria). Roa Bastos, who had suffered so badly in Paraguay, found a new champion. Nadine Gordimer, who had supported *Index* from the beginning, published a story about the romantic dilemmas of a secret policeman in South Africa. In Europe, Samuel Beckett became so engaged with the plight of Václav Havel that he dedicated a short play, 'Catastrophe', to his fellow playwright and allowed *Index* to publish it in its pages, another notable scoop. By the end of the 1980s, the idea of standing up for the abstract idea of 'intellectual freedom' by reporting censorship and publishing banned writing had become a recognised part of the common discourse within the libertarian community.

The influence of *Index* on the literary world has been at once subtle and impossible to overstate. In my mind, there is no doubt that its example became an inspiration to those British publishers, like Faber, Penguin and Picador, who (especially in the 1970s and 1980s) published banned or oppressed writers such as Milan Kundera, Václav Havel and Josef Skvorecky. The literature that came from behind the Iron Curtain added a new dimension to the reading of the West. Translations of novels like *The Book of Laughter and Forgetting* were so exceptional that the book would briefly become, ex officio, as it were, almost a part of the Anglo-American literary tradition.

The institutional importance of *Index* is hard to overstate because, in the words of André Gide, good sentiments do not usually generate good literature. Just because a writer is committed to fighting injustice in his or her society, there's no guarantee that his or her work will have artistic value. But once the role of literature as 'witness' is established in the minds of the public, it makes it more difficult to dissociate literary merit and the social or political value of the text. *Index* provided a forum for banned writers to demonstrate the role of literature, both good and less good, as unsubmissive, contrarian, transcendent and instinctively transgressive.

Perhaps it was as well that the *Index* model was so firmly set by Spender and its founders. After 1989, the strength and security of WSI (notwithstanding a constant search for sponsors) was crucial. The fall of the Wall and the disintegration of the Soviet Union gave every indication that the raison d'être of *Index* – opposing Soviet oppression – had been trumped by History.

In fact, the reverse was the case. Writers and free expression continued to be persecuted worldwide. Russia did not cease to be despotic with the disbanding of the KGB. In some ways, the condition of everyday life for

Demonstrators, holding candles and pictures of murdered
Russian journalist Anna Politkovskaya, Helsinki, 24 November 2006
Credit: Mikko Stig/Rex Features

19

Russian writers grew significantly worse, and certainly far more dangerous. The war in Chechnya gave the authorities a new pretext to crush free journalism. Anna Politovskaya became just one of many who turned to *Index* to make her plight better understood in the West.

With the millennium, meanwhile, the rise of the internet and the IT revolution inherent in the development of digital communications offered a new challenge. The old barriers to state control were coming down. Frontiers that had once been impenetrable were suddenly porous. Secret policemen could continue to terrorise writers, printers and publishers, but it was much harder to stop the free flow of information on the worldwide web. What place would *Index* have in the new world order of 'free' content shaped by Google, Wikipedia and Amazon? The answer, of course, is as a research institution, a memory bank and a continuing moral example, along with publishing online as well as in print.

Index in the new century has made the fight for 'intellectual freedom' normative as well as liberating. WSI remains the tool of one very simple, good idea. Its historical board members are unchanged: Milton, Paine, Wilkes, Zola and, possibly, Orwell. *Index* knows that such an achievement is not lightly won. The history of state repression shows that the individual writer and artist and scholar is vulnerable on his own. He, or she, needs the committed support of independent organisations that cannot be crushed by state terror. Furthermore, the plight of writers especially should not be at the mercy of intellectual fashion or the caprice of a Twitter feed. Free expression needs its gatekeepers: publishers, editors, booksellers, and independent columnists. And this community needs a place to meet, a forum for ideas and debate. This is what *Index* provides. More serious than Twitter; better organised than Facebook, it's a forum that can exploit the social media, but not become its prisoner.

In the 21st century, this can be virtual, articulated through Google or Wikipedia. But it also needs to be orchestrated by people, standing apart from fashionable trends, who understand the nuances of the fight for intellectual freedom and who know what they are talking about. This, in a sentence, is the unique *Index* proposition: ideas honestly and freely expressed and writers worldwide uninhibited by the censorship of the mind or tyrannical restrictions on the printed word. ❐

©Robert McCrum
41(1): 12/20
DOI: 10.1177/0306422012439498
www.indexoncensorship.org

Robert McCrum is an associate editor of the *Observer*. He has been a member of the advisory board of *Index on Censorship* since 1983

Caption *page 15*
Sir Stephen Spender
Credit: Caroline Austin

Winner of the Nobel Prize for Literature
Winner of the Booker Prize

NADINE GORDIMER

NO TIME LIKE THE PRESENT

'Gordimer has undoubtedly become one of the World's Great Writers ... her rootedness in a political time, place and faith has never dimmed her complex gifts as an artist'
INDEPENDENT

'Nadine Gordimer has earned a place among the few novelists who really matter'
OBSERVER

'Gordimer's stark sentences and emotional depth make most modern fiction seem trivial'
THE TIMES

'Nadine Gordimer writes of blacks and whites, but her steady, unblinking eye sees something grey there. You could call it human nature, and you would be right'
DAILY TELEGRAPH

AVAILABLE NOW IN ALL GOOD BOOKSTORES AND ONLINE

B L O O M S B U R Y
www.bloomsbury.com/nadinegordimer

e Available as an **eBook**

`GOD KEEP ME FROM GOING MAD´

Alexander Solzhenitsyn

This is the first ever publication in English of verse passage in question is an extract from a longer a composed in 1950-53 while Solzhenitsyn was serving camp in North Kazakhstan. This camp formed the set celebrated novel, One Day in the Life of Ivan Denis *quoted in a* samizdat *article on the novel called* Iva Writer's Spiritual Mission *by Venyamin Teush, a colleague and close friend of Solzhenitsyn. Teush psuedonym D. Blagov.*

There never was, nor will be, a world of brightr
A frozen footcloth is the scarf that binds my f
Fights over porridge, the ganger's constant grip
And day follows day follows day, and no end t
. . . .

My feeble pick strikes sparks from the frozen e
And the sun stares down unblinking from the s
But the world *is* here! And will be! The daily r
Suffices. But man is not to be prisoned in the
To write! To write now, without delay
Not in heated wrath, but with cy

TIGHT IS THE CIRCLE

This was the first ever publication in English of verse by **Alexander Solzhenitsyn,** written while the author was in the gulag in Kazakhstan

The poem that follows is an extract from a longer autobiographical work composed in 1950-53, 'The Road', while Solzhenitsyn was in the camp that formed the setting of his celebrated novel One Day in the Life of Ivan Denisovich. *The verse was quoted in a* samizdat *article on the novel called 'Ivan Denisovich and the Writer's Spiritual Mission' by Venyamin Teush, a former schoolteacher colleague and close friend of Solzhenitsyn. Teush signed it with the pseudonym D Blagov.*

There never was, nor will be, a world of brightness!
A frozen footcloth is the scarf that binds my face.
Fights over porridge, the ganger's constant griping
And day follows day follows day, and no end to this dreary fate.

My feeble pick strikes sparks from the frozen earth.
And the sun stares down unblinking from the sky.
But the world *is* here! And will be! The daily round
Suffices. But man is not to be prisoned in the day.
To write! To write now, without delay,
Not in heated wrath, but with cool and clear understanding.
The millstones of my thoughts can hardly turn,
Too rare the flicker of light in my aching soul.
Yes, tight is the circle around us tautly drawn,
But my verses will burst their bonds and freely roam
And I can guard, perhaps, beyond their reach,
In rhythmic harmony this hard–won gift of speech.

And then they can grope my body in vain –
'Here I am. All yours. Look hard. Not a line...
Our indestructible memory, by wonder divine,
Is beyond the reach of your butcher's hands!'

My labour of love! Year after year with me you will grow,
Year after year you will tread the prisoner's path.
The day will come when you warm not me alone,
Nor me alone embrace with a shiver of wrath.
Let the stanzas throb – but no whisper let slip,
Let them hammer away – not a twitch of the lip,
Let your eyes not gleam in another's presence
And let no one see, let no one see
You put pencil to paper.
From every corner I am stalked by prison –
God keep me from going mad!

I do not write my verses for idle pleasure,
Nor from a sense of energy to burn.
Nor out of mischief, to evade their searches,
Do I carry them past my captors in my brain.
The free flow of my verse is dearly bought,
I have paid a cruel price for my poet's rights:
The barren sacrifice of all her youth
And ten cold solitary years for my wife –

The unuttered cries of children still unborn,
My mother's death, toiling in gaunt starvation,
The madness of prison cells, midnight interrogations,
Autumn's sticky red clay in an opencast mine,
The secret, slow and silent erosive force
Of winters laying bricks, of summers feeding the furnace –
Oh, if this were but the sum of the price paid for my verse!
But those others paid the price with their lives,
Immured in the silence of Solovki, drowned in thunder of waves,
Or shot without trial in Vorkuta's polar night.

Love and warmth and their executed cries
Have combined in my breast to carve

From the Archive 1972

The receptive metre of this sorrowful tale,
These few poor thousand incapacious lines.
Oh, hopeless labour! Can you really pay the price?
Do you think to redeem the pledge with a single life?
For what an age has my country been so poor
In women's happy laughter, so very rich
In poets' lamentations!
Verse verse – for all that we have lost,
A drop of scented resin in the razed forest!
But this is all I live for! On its wings
I transport my feeble body through prison walls
And one day, in distant exile dim,
Biding my time, I will free my tortured memory from its thrall:
On paper, birchbark, in a blackened bottle rolled,
I will consign my tale to the forest leaves,
Or to a drift of shifting snow.

But what if beforehand they give me poisoned bread?
Or if darkness beclouds my mind at last?
Oh, let me die *there*! Let it not be here!
God keep me from going mad! ❑

Translated by Michael Scammell

©Alexander Solzhenitsyn
41(1): 22/25
DOI: 10.1177/0306422012438321
www.indexoncensorship.org

This poem first appeared in *Index on Censorship* Volume 1, Number 2, Summer 1972

THELONGVIEW

Michael Scammell, founding editor of *Index*, on the landmark publication of the Soviet Union's number one dissident, Solzhenitsyn

During my years as editor of *Index*, our sympathies were always with individual writers and intellectuals, rather than movements – the word 'dissident' still sums them up best – and we made a point of publishing original work by as many authors as we could (we had two Nobel Prize winners in our first year). In fact, we published the Soviet Union's number one dissident, Solzhenitsyn, even before he won the Nobel Prize. In our first issue we carried a hitherto unknown prose poem, 'Means of Transport'; in our second an excerpt from a long, unpublished autobiographical poem, 'The Road'; and in our double issue at the end of the year, Solzhenitsyn's Nobel Prize speech.

The following year we had only one long article on Solzhenitsyn – an interview with two western correspondents – but along with the rest of the world we followed the sensational news that the KGB had acquired a copy of *The Gulag Archipelago* after torturing one of the typists and that Solzhenitsyn had gone into hiding, which was followed by his arrest and his deportation to the West in February 1974.

By this time I had been involuntarily drawn into Solzhenitsyn's circle myself. *Index*'s publication of his prose poem and the news that we planned to publish an excerpt from 'The Road', neither of which had appeared anywhere in print, had alarmed him, and at one point he had asked me, through a dissident friend of mine, to stop publication. He feared his works were being circulated by the KGB as a provocation in order to frame him, but I was able to show they came from genuine *samizdat*. There were more desultory contacts of this nature, and then a Swiss lawyer, Dr Fritz Heeb, who was acting as Solzhenitsyn's literary agent in the West, got in touch with me. He sent a Russian copy of Solzhenitsyn's *Letter to the Leaders* (as it was originally called) and asked if I could begin to make arrangements for its publication in English. It was a call to the Soviet leaders to liberalise their system, ease censorship, and begin the transition to a form of limited democracy. It was a sensational proposal, which Solzhenitsyn had written well before his exile, but had kept secret in the vain hope the government would respond.

Solzhenitsyn was deported and arrived at Dr Heeb's home in Zurich before I could begin, and he sent instructions for his *Letter* to be published as soon as possible. At 15,000 words it was too long for the magazine, and we decided to publish it as a book. Our tiny staff of four at *Index* immediately swung into action. I had planned to do the translation myself, but there was no time, so I asked a friend, Hilary Sternberg, to translate it, and she worked frantically day and night to get it finished. I also knew that the *Letter* was hot news and deserved extended press coverage. The *Sunday Times* in London seized on the opportunity and published our translation of the *Letter* in full. The *New York Times,* however, double-crossed us. Having turned down my offer of the text, they sent a correspondent to Solzhenitsyn's Russian-language publisher in Paris and, using my name, obtained a copy of the Russian and did a translation of their own.

Hilary Sternberg, helped by our assistant editor, George Theiner, and our distribution manager, Philip Spender (with Philip's wife, Jane, reading the proofs), pulled out all the stops to get the translation finished and our book out. It was printed and distributed by Collins (Fontana handled the paperback) and sold tens of thousands of copies, bringing in a very large sum of money. We had hoped to be able to keep some of it to support *Index*, and were disappointed when Solzhenitsyn insisted that all the proceeds should go to him, but I myself benefitted greatly from the enterprise. In the course of the next few months I went to New York to edit the English translation of volume one of *The Gulag Archipelago,* began a translation of Solzhenitsyn's memoir, *The Oak and the Calf* (which I later handed over to his translator Harry Willetts), visited Solzhenitsyn in Zurich, and got his grudging agreement 'not to oppose' my idea of writing his biography. ❏

©Michael Scammell
41(1): 26/27
DOI: 10.1177/0306422012439506
www.indexoncensorship.org

Michael Scammell founded *Index* in 1972 and edited it until 1980. He is the author of *Solzhenitsyn: a Biography,* and *Koestler: The Indispensable Intellectual* (Faber)

WORD POWER

Aung San Suu Kyi

The gift of speech is the most effective instrument for human communication. The ability to communicate enables us to establish links across time and space, to learn to understand different civilisations and cultures, to extend knowledge both vertically and horizontally, to promote the arts and sciences. It also helps to bridge gaps in understanding between peoples and nations, to put an end to old enmities, to achieve détente, to cultivate new fellowships. Speech is words strung together to allow human beings to articulate their thoughts and emotions. Words allow us to express our feelings, to record our experiences, to concretise our ideas, to push outwards the frontiers of intellectual exploration. Words can move hearts, words can change perceptions, words can set nations and peoples in powerful motion. Words are an essential part of the expression of our humanness. To curb and shackle freedom of speech and expression is to cripple the basic right to realise our full potential as human beings.

Can freedom of speech be abused? Since historical times it has been recognised that words can hurt as well as heal, that we have a responsibility to use our verbal skills in the right way. What is the 'right' way? The Ten Commandments of the Old Testament include an injunction against the bearing of false witness. Misusing the gift of speech to deceive or harm others is generally seen as unacceptable. Buddhism teaches that there are four verbal acts that constitute 'tainted failure in living': uttering deliberate lies for one's own sake, for the sake of others, or for some material advantage; uttering words that cause dissension, that is, creating discord among those united and inciting still more those who are in discord; speaking harshly and abusively, causing anger and distraction of mind in others; indulging in talk that is inadvisable, unrestrained and harmful.

Modern laws reflect the preoccupations of our ancients. Perjury, slander and libel, incitement to communal hatred, incitement to violence – all these are indictable offences in many countries today. The recognition of the negative consequences of misusing our gift of speech has not, however, been matched by an awareness of the detrimental effects of stifling free speech.

It is most generally in societies where the plinth of power is narrow that freedom of speech is perceived as a threat to the existing order. When speaking out against existing wrongs and injustices is disallowed, society is deprived of a vital impetus towards positive change and renewal. Censorship laws that ostensibly protect society from iniquitous influences generally achieve little that is positive. The most usual result is a pervasive atmosphere of uncertainty and fear that strangles innovative thought.

It was only in the 20th century that freedom of expression began to be recognised as a basic human right. Today, freedom of speech and expression remain tenuous or even unknown in many nations that are signatories to the United Nations Charter on Human Rights. As in the distant past, it is those in positions of power and influence who stand against the freedom to articulate common grievances and aspirations.

It has been rightly pointed out that what is most important is not so much freedom *of* speech as freedom *after* speech. Through long years of authoritarian rule, members of the movement for democracy in Burma have been punished for speaking out in protest against violations of human rights and abuses of power. The few who spoke out were articulating the silent protest of the many who had been cowed into submission. To stand as a few against the juggernaut of power is hard. It was the solidarity of like-minded people, at home and abroad, that strengthened our advocates of freedom of speech.

An advocate of freedom of expression is necessarily also a practitioner. The basic law for those who want to defend freedom of expression is that they must demonstrate their commitment by practising what they preach. When we speak out for our right to freedom of speech we begin to exercise it. When we write about our right to freedom of expression we begin to practise it. There can be no theoretical advocacy of these freedoms, there can only be practical, practising advocacy. ❏

©Aung San Suu Kyi
41(1): 28/29
DOI: 10.1177/0306422012438641
www.indexoncensorship.org

Aung San Suu Kyi is leader of the National League for Democracy. She was awarded the Nobel Peace Prize in 1991

Aung San Suu Kyi leaves the district election commission after registering as
a candidate for the forthcoming election, Rangoon, Burma, 18 January 2012
Credit: Khin Maung Win/AP/Press Association

contents

ANATOMY OF DICTATORSHIP

As Burma marked 50 years of independence, veteran editor **Adam Michnik** asked whether it would follow the same path to transformation as Poland

The unreconciled will always resist where systematic lies and violence prevail. They know the taste of hypocrisy; the smell of fear; the touch of cruelty. And with unfailing instinct, too, they recognise their fellows: their heroism, determination and courage.

In Rangoon, I heard the arguments of the defenders of the military dictatorship. They spoke of 'reasons of state' and 'irresponsible, destabilising elements'.

And I saw people so paralysed by fear of the police that they would not speak to a foreigner.

Not least, I saw functionaries of the Burmese security services who would not allow anyone to enter the home of Nobel Prize winner and leader of the National league for Democracy (NLD) Aung San Suu Kyi.

Looking at Burma, I thought of Poland. Thinking of the Polish experience, I saw Burma. I belong to the 'unreconciled'. I remember well what dictatorship means. I am not in the least tempted to relativism about what I experienced then: the abject humiliation and the fear. Burma has its 'hope', its 'Solidarnosc' in the NLD. It went through its August 1980 (the two-week strike in the Gdansk shipyard that led to the birth of Solidarity) in 1988. It has been through its martial law; it has its WRON (Jaruzelski's Military Council for the Salvation of the Nation) called the SLORC (State Law and Order Restoration Council, reborn in November 1997 as the State Law and Development Council.) It has its Lech Walesa in Daw Aung San Suu Kyi. It does not yet have its General Wojciech Jaruzelski mark 1989 (the year of the Polish Round Table at which all sectors of society met), although it does have its Jaruzelski mark 1981 (the declaration of martial law in Poland). Will a Burmese Jaruzelski willing to open a Round Table emerge?

'The reformer abandons the logic of revolution for the logic of negotiation.'
Shipyard strike, Gdansk, Poland, 1980
Credit: Peter Marlow/Magnum

The NLD won an overwhelming victory in the 1990 elections only to have victory snatched away by the military who remained in charge as they had done since 1962. NLD leaders were confined to prison. I visited NLD leaders at night and in secret. While Pawel, my colleague from Gazeta Wyborcza, kept muttering 'Junta shit', I remembered the police blockade of Lech Walesa's flat in Gdansk, the ubiquitous presence of the secret police, house searches, detentions and arrests, the anxiety of neighbours and later their discreetly expressed admiration. Déjà-vu, I thought. In Rangoon I felt 20 years younger.

Dictatorship emerges from the weaknesses of democracy and from a lack of consensus on the rules of the democratic game. Those who muddy the waters in the name of social justice, historical truth or the battle against corruption generally do so for serious reasons. The Bolsheviks sought to end World War I and promised radical agricultural reform; the Nazis intended to control inflation and overcome anarchy, unemployment and the stifling humiliation of the Treaty of Versailles.

Jaruzelski aimed to stem the progressive disintegration of the Communist state and secure Poland from the threat of 'fraternal intervention'. The Burmese generals sought to guarantee the unity of a country torn by ethnic warfare and bring safety to city streets they claimed were ruled by gangs of thugs. For many people the distinction between order and chaos carries greater weight than the difference between democracy and dictatorship.

Dictatorship is security as well as fear. It is liberation from the need to make choices. Others decide: as for me, I am free of the threat of risk and the burden of responsibility; my obedience is the key to happiness and a career. But security also means danger. The institution which prompted the greatest fear in Communist Poland was the Ministry of Public Security. The security apparatus was a state within the state: its agents and informers became the bearers of an all-pervading fear. Laughter died, conversations slipped into silence. Safety became transfigured into danger: a security service colonel was more loathed than the leader of a band of criminals.

In a dictatorship, the security chief is as unassailable as the head of an underworld mafia in times of freedom. But who is more to be feared? Those aspiring to a role in public life are more likely to be fearful of the security colonel; those who want a quiet life will be more concerned about the mafia terrorising the city in a fragile, corrupt and helpless parliamentary democracy. As a rule, dictatorships guarantee safe streets and terror of the doorbell. In a democracy the streets may be unsafe after dark, but the most likely visitor in the early hours will be the milkman.

Democracy is uncertainty, risk and responsibility, but it seldom enforces its policies through violence. Dictatorship means violence daily; it is fear, humiliation and silence. But it is the charm of dictatorship that it liberates people from responsibility: the state answers for everything. You cease to be a citizen and become state property.

★★★

Every dictatorship is controlled by economics. If the economy collapses, the desperate come out onto the streets demanding bread. When the police begin to shoot they demand bread and freedom. If the economy develops well, there will be a limited period of peace, but people whose elementary needs – and particularly their children's – are met will eventually seek civic freedoms. Such is the natural order of things.

Economic collapse leads to revolt born of despair, economic growth to rebellion born of aspiration. This rebellion also permeates the inner reaches of the dictatorship. Increasing numbers of people from the ruling apparatus find they no longer want to be sitting on a time-bomb. They are tempted to introduce a rationalised system of democratic reform. Reforms introduced from within the dictatorship are invariably intended to change everything so that nothing changes. The dialectic of change depends on that singular encounter between a reformer from within the dictatorship and a reformer from the opposition. In Burma I met both: people from the junta responsible for the crimes of martial law and long-term political prisoners from the opposition.

★★★

Dictatorship hates reform and loves 'development and improvement'. But, despite everything, reform keeps knocking at the gate. Because, at some quite arbitrary moment, people rebel. Police squadrons disperse the crowd. There are victims: the wounded, the arrested and the dead.

The people have their martyrs. Police batons and arrests act as agents of integration and new leaders are its hallmark. And though later they may be arrested, smeared and abused, they remain a sign of hope in the collective memory. Solzhenitsyn and Sakharov, Walesa and Havel – and Aung San Sui Kyi. Social resistance is no longer a shapeless river of stones spewed up from riot-riven streets onto government buildings; there are leaders now to articulate political proposals with whom the authorities can negotiate. If – and this is the crux – the will is there on both sides.

The thing to do is to wait for the Great Explosion

And so the arguments begin, in the corridors of power and among the opposition as well as in the democratic world without. Inside the establishment 'men of concrete' talk of closing ranks in the face of an outside threat. Any change will be read as a sign of weakness, they argue. The opposition want only to destroy us. Its success will lead to chaos and collapse, and take us to prison or the hangman's noose. It will be a gift for foreign enemies, whom the opposition in this country represent.

And government reformers are unconscious tools of the destruction the opposition seek to wreak. How can reformers now persuade their comrades in the dictatorial camp that the more inflexible they remain, the harder they are working to self-destruct? Blind faith in the principles of traditional doctrine has to lead to rebellion, bloodshed, chaos and the collapse of the state.

The result of the debate between 'men of concrete' and the reformers is also determined by signals from the democratic opposition and from abroad. The opposition – previously held together by the firmness of its resistance to the dictatorship – begins to break up. Should it focus on public protest or seek routes to negotiation? Should it demand punishment for the dictators or agree to compromise, reconciliation and reform?

At the critical moment, that is the dilemma. The 'revolutionaries' continue to repeat their arguments: the dictatorship has innocent blood on its hands, it is an absolute evil and its people are the carriers of that evil. The evil must be exposed and destroyed and its carriers appropriately punished. That is what justice demands; that is our duty to the victims of the dictatorship. Any attempt at compromise with evil is a gesture of support for it, the destruction of the purity of the 'idea', moral fraud and political folly. The thing to do is to wait for the Great Explosion when people take to the streets. That is the time to stand up and lead, and overturn the dictatorship. Only then will truth and liberty triumph, justice be victorious, virtue rewarded, treachery and transgression punished.

'Reformers' see things differently. We could be waiting for the Great Explosion for a long time, they say. It holds immense risk: social suicide, civil war, new wrongs and new victims. Life is short, the country is going to waste and the people have not yet recovered from earlier revolutions. That is why negotiations with yesterday's enemy must be undertaken, to find ways to a peaceful dismantling of the dictatorship, and to compromise.

To the revolutionary, compromise is opportunism and lack of principle. To the reformer, it is essential. The reformer abandons the logic of revolution for the logic of negotiation. Earlier, he had sought out everything that divided him from the dictatorship; now he must search for whatever they have in common. He is exposed to allegations of betrayal. For it is in the nature of compromise that some principles are abandoned; that victory isn't absolute; that yesterday's enemy must be allowed full citizen's rights and a place under the sun. If, in the dictatorial establishment, the 'men of concrete' prevail, there can be no hope of compromise; nor if the revolutionaries do so in society. But if reformers from both sides emerge victorious, the country has won its prize on the lottery.

The Poles won their lottery in Spring 1989. And what of Burma?

In foreign capitals, the transformations of a creaking dictatorship are carefully watched. Tactics are considered: political boycott and economic sanction, or flexibility and 'politically realistic' silence on human rights. Or perhaps the carrot and stick, pressuring the dictatorship to tolerate the expansion of civil society.

If pressure from abroad — economic, political and diplomatic — is in the interest of the reformers from the power camp and reformers from the democratic position, the chances for a peaceful transformation are very real. That was the formula in the Polish Velvet Revolution. No one gives up power faced with the spectre of a guillotine. People from the regime must have some guarantees of safety. Otherwise they will defend their power to the end, drowning the country in blood. Only after their total defeat will real justice triumph — amid burned-out cities, orphaned families, thousands of newly dug graves.

Negotiation brings disappointment, bitterness, a sense of injustice and unpaid debts. But it spares the victims: those who are disappointed are at least still living. Negotiations are possible when democratic resistance is strong enough for the dictatorship not to destroy it, and while the dictatorship itself is strong enough for the democratic opposition not to overthrow it overnight. The country has its chance in the weakness of both sides. ❏

Translated by Irena Maryniak
©Adam Michnik
41(1): 32/39
DOI: 10.1177/0306422012438644
www.indexoncensorship.org

Adam Michnik is editor-in-chief of *Gazeta Wyborcza*, the leading Polish daily, and was a key figure in the events that led to the fall of communism in Poland. This is an edited version of an article first published in *Index on Censorship* Volume 27, Number 1, January/February 1998

Letter from *Václav Havel to* Index on Censorship, *August 1989*
(facing page)

Thank you, friends

The Central European researcher of *Index on Censorship* recently received the following letter from the Czechoslovak playwright Václav Havel, who was writing from his country cottage in Hrádeček, Northern Bohemia.

'Dear friend, Not until now — the 7th and 8th of August — has my dramatic life given me the opportunity to dig deeper into the mountain of correspondence from recent months. In it I found letters about the British collection from which a new computer was bought for me. I have it here in Hrádeček, am using it, and would like to express my profound thanks to all those who made donations. The best way I think, to do this would be through the pages of *Index on Censorship* which, as far as I know, was the most active organiser of the collection. So please be kind enough to publish the following:'

My dear colleagues and friends,
Thank you all for contributing money to buy me a new computer. I feel that this public and demonstrative act of solidarity and, at the same time, of protest against the groundless confiscation of my previous computer by the Czechoslovak police, was extremely important. It was not only an immediate help and reinforcement for me. It was above all a lesson to the authoritarian Czechoslovak regime which was obliged to realise that none of its wrongdoings and injustices would remain unanswered. What you did was without any doubt one of the reasons why my first computer was, after all, returned to me.

I shall consult with friends and pass it on to a colleague who will be able to use it most effectively.

Once again, thank you from the bottom of my heart,

Yours,

Václav Havel, Hrádeček, 8 August 1989

Putting out the fire

not running for re-election … voted against the resolution. Said the Republican Gordon Humphrey, 'This … amounts to an exercise in silliness and even a bit of hypocrisy.' In the House, there were … votes.

On 27 June, President Bush called a conference to announce his support for a constitutional amendment banning desecration of the flag. 'Flag burning is wrong, dead wrong.' he declared, despite suggestions that he had been wrapping himself in the flag since his presidential campaign. 'I will uphold our … to dissent, but flag burning goes too far.'

Public opinion polls … following the Court decision showed … support for Bush's position. By 4 July, 4 states passed resolutions urging an amendment; at least 10 others were considering … measures.

By mid-July, however, when Senate Republican leader Bob Dole introduced … amendment in the Senate with the support of the President and 22 senators (16 less than the number needed to pass), newspapers were already reporting flagging public interest in the flag issue.

A week later, Joseph Biden, chair of the Senate Judiciary Committee, introduced a bill which would make it a crime to desecrate a flag. Biden's bill and a similar one introduced in the House are attempts to sidestep free speech issues by outlawing actions without mentioning motivations — part of flag desecration that the … court determined is protected by the First Amendment ● Sue Levenson

ENEMIES OF FREE SPEECH

Freedom of expression is now viewed as an enemy of liberty as much as its friend. **Kenan Malik** considers the fallout from a watershed

'I have definitely become a free speech fundamentalist,' says Flemming Rose. Perhaps that should not be surprising. It was, after all, Rose who helped launch the Danish cartoon controversy in 2005 as culture editor of the newspaper *Jyllands-Posten*. He had picked up on a story about the difficulties that children's author Kåre Bluitgen had faced in finding an illustrator for a book he was writing on Islam. Every illustrator whom Bluitgen had contacted had been worried that he would end up like Theo van Gogh, the Dutch filmmaker ritually murdered on the streets of Amsterdam by a Muslim incensed by his anti-Islamic films. Rose wanted, he said, to see 'how deep this self-censorship lies in the Danish public'. So he set a challenge to Danish cartoonists: draw a caricature of the Prophet Mohammed and we will publish a selection in *Jyllands-Posten*.

Rose approached 42 cartoonists, 12 of whom accepted the challenge. Their caricatures, including Kurt Westergaard's infamous image of the prophet wearing a turban in the form of a bomb, were published in *Jyllands-Posten* on 30 September 2005. 'The modern secular society,' Rose wrote in a commentary, 'is rejected by some Muslims. They demand a special position, insisting on special consideration of their own religious feelings. It is incompatible with contemporary democracy and freedom of speech, where you must be ready to put up with insults, mockery and ridicule.'

To Rose's critics, the very act of publishing the cartoons, and of provoking Muslims into a response, was irresponsible, even racist. In their eyes Rose has always been a 'free speech fundamentalist', and not in a good way. Not so, Rose told me. When he published the cartoons, he believed in free speech, but he did not have a deep understanding of the subject. It was the controversy itself that made him think about the real meaning of freedom of expression, and challenged many of his preconceptions.

The contemporary debate about free speech has been shaped by two key confrontations over the past two decades. The first was the Salman Rushdie affair, the second the Danish cartoons controversy. The controversy over *The Satanic Verses* was a cultural and political watershed, the storm through which many of the issues that have become the defining problems of our age first emerged into popular consciousness – the nature of Islam, and its relationship to the West, the meaning of multiculturalism, the fear of terrorism, the boundaries of tolerance in a liberal society, the limits of free speech in a plural world, and so on.

If the controversy over *The Satanic Verses* provided a glimpse of the world as it would come to be, the furore over the Danish cartoons helped lay bare the anatomy of the world as it had become. 'The context was very different,' says Rose about the two controversies. 'I followed the Rushdie affair, but at that time the big global story was the breakdown of communism in Eastern Europe.' The 'debate about migration, integration and diversity' is very different now than it was in 1989, he believes, and 'far more complex'.

Perhaps the biggest difference, however, between the Rushdie affair and the cartoons controversy lay less in the context than in the attitudes, particularly the attitudes of liberal intellectuals towards free speech and the idea of giving offence. In 1989 there had been much equivocation by politicians and intellectuals, but with one or two exceptions, such as John le Carré, who claimed that 'there is no law in life or nature that says great religions may be insulted with impunity', and Germaine Greer, who allegedly declared that 'jail is a good place for writers', no one seriously doubted Rushdie's right to publish his novel. There was little equivocation over the Danish cartoons, just a widespread acceptance that *Jyllands-Posten* had been in the wrong, and even more so the newspapers and magazines that had republished the cartoons. Writers and artists, many insisted, had a responsibility to desist from giving offence and upsetting religious sensibilities.

'I understand your concerns,' Louise Arbour, the UN High Commissioner for Human Rights, told delegates at an Organisation of Islamic Conference summit in Mecca in 2005, 'and would like to emphasise that I regret any statement or act that could express a lack of respect for the religion of others.' The European Union, too, expressed 'regret' about the publication of the cartoons. 'These kinds of drawings can add to the growing Islamophobia in Europe,' claimed Franco Frattini, EU Commissioner for Justice, Freedom and Security. Former US President Bill Clinton condemned 'these totally outrageous cartoons against Islam' and feared that anti-Semitism had been replaced by anti-Islamic prejudice.

The difference in attitudes revealed how the very landscape of free speech had been transformed. Peter Mayer had been CEO of Penguin, Rushdie's publishers at the time of the fatwa. He talked publicly about those events in an interview he gave for my book *From Fatwa to Jihad*. Early on the morning of Valentine's Day 1989, Mayer received a call from Patrick Wright, Penguin's head of sales in London. Had he seen the headlines about the fatwa, Wright asked him. 'What's a fatwa?' asked a bemused Mayer. It was not just the idea of a fatwa that was new; neither Mayer nor Penguin had even begun to think about the issues that were soon to dominate their lives. 'We had never had to have this kind of discussion before,' Mayer observed. 'Today there is a constant stream of discussion about multiculturalism and minority rights and sharia law. Not then. We had never had to think about free speech or about why we were publishers.'

The fatwa ushered in not just a new kind of debate but a new kind of violence. Salman Rushdie was forced into hiding for almost a decade. Translators and publishers were assaulted and even murdered. In July 1991, Hitoshi Igarashi, a Japanese professor of literature and translator of *The Satanic Verses*, was knifed to death on the campus of Tsukuba University. That same month, another translator of Rushdie's novel, the Italian Ettore

1979 – Iran

The Shah is forced into exile and Ayatollah Khomeini returns. On 1 April, following a referendum, an Islamic Republic is declared and strict regulations on free speech, artistic expression and women's conduct are introduced.

Flemming Rose, 3 February 2006. Photos provided by the photo agency ready blurred.
Credit: Julian Simmonds/Rex Features

Capriolo, was beaten up and stabbed in his Milan apartment. In October 1993, William Nygaard, the Norwegian publisher of *The Satanic Verses*, was shot three times and left for dead outside his home in Oslo. Bookshops were firebombed for stocking the novel.

Mayer himself was subject to a vicious campaign of hatred and intimidation. 'I had letters delivered to me written in blood,' he remembered. 'I had telephone calls in the middle of the night, saying not just that they would kill me but that they would take my daughter and smash her head against a concrete wall. Vile stuff.'

And yet neither Mayer nor Penguin had countenanced backing down. 'I told the board, "You have to take the long view. Any climbdown now will only encourage future terrorist attacks by individuals or groups offended for whatever reason by other books that we or any publisher might publish. If we capitulate, there will be no publishing as we know it."' Mayer and his colleagues recognised that 'what we did now affected much more than simply the fate of this one book. How we responded to the controversy over *The Satanic Verses* would affect the future of free inquiry, without which there would be no publishing as we knew it, but also, by extension, no civil society as we knew it. We all came to agree that all we could do, as individuals or as a company, was to uphold the principles that underlay our profession and which, since the invention of movable type, have brought it respect. We were publishers. I thought that meant something. We all did.'

Nygaard, too, was resolute in his refusal to give way. He spent weeks in hospital, followed by months of rehabilitation. It was two years before he could fully use his arms and legs again. 'Journalists kept asking me, "Will you stop publishing *The Satanic Verses*?"', he told me in an interview. 'I said, "Absolutely not."'

Mayer and Nygaard belonged to a world in which the defence of free speech was seen as an irrevocable duty. That world no longer exists, swept away in part by the reverberations of the Rushdie affair. In the world to which Mayer and Nygaard belonged, speech was seen as an inherent good, the fullest extension of which was a necessary condition for the elucidation of truth, the expression of moral autonomy, the maintenance of social progress and the development of other liberties. Of course, the traditional liberal defence of free speech was shot through with hypocrisy. Defenders of free expression were often wont to cite a whole host of harms – from the incitement to hatred to threats to national security, from the promotion of blasphemy to the spread of slander – as reasons to curtail speech that they found particularly obnoxious. Yet however hypocritical liberal arguments may sometimes have seemed, and notwithstanding the fact that most free speech advocates accepted that the line had to be drawn somewhere, there was nevertheless an acknowledgement that speech was truly important and that restrictions on free speech should be the exception rather than the norm.

By the time of the Danish cartoons, free speech had come to be seen as a threat to liberty as much as its shield. By its very nature, many now argued, speech damaged basic freedoms. It was not intrinsically a good, but inherently a problem, because speech inevitably offends and harms. Speech, therefore, had to be restrained, not in exceptional circumstances but all the time and everywhere, especially in diverse societies with a variety of deeply held views and beliefs. Censorship, and self-censorship, had to become the norm.

We live in a world, so the argument ran, in which there were deep-seated conflicts between cultures embodying different values. For such diverse societies to function and to be fair, we needed to show respect for other peoples, cultures and viewpoints. Social justice required not just that individuals are treated as political equals, but also that their cultural beliefs were given equal recognition and respect. The avoidance of cultural pain has therefore come to be regarded as more important than the abstract right to freedom of expression. As the British sociologist Tariq Modood put it, 'If people are to occupy the same political space without conflict, they mutually have to limit the extent to which they subject each other's fundamental beliefs to criticism.' Or, as the Muslim philosopher and spokesman for the Bradford Council of Mosques Shabbir Akhtar claimed at the height of the Rushdie affair, 'Self-censorship is a meaningful demand in a world of varied and passionately held convictions. What Rushdie publishes about Islam is not just his business. It is everyone's – not least every Muslim's – business.'

Rose captures this transformation well in his description of how the meaning of tolerance has been remade. Tolerance, Rose told me, should be 'about the ability to be exposed, and to accept things you don't like', the ability 'to live with what you find distasteful. What you don't like, what you abhor'. But the concept has, in recent years, been 'turned on its head'. Tolerance, he explains, 'is no longer about the ability to tolerate things for which we do not care, but more about the ability to keep quiet and refrain from saying things that others may not care to hear. *Jyllands-Posten* was criticised for being intolerant. That suggests that tolerance is something demanded of the one who speaks, or the one who draws the cartoon, or writes the novel, rather than something demanded of the one who listens, or looks at the cartoon or reads the novel. That's why I say that tolerance has been turned on its head.'

Tolerance, in other words, used to mean the acceptance of diversity and difference. Today it has come to mean the very opposite: the refusal to accept diversity and difference, the insistence that others abide by my views of what is acceptable and unacceptable. Once every group insists that other groups have to respect its boundaries then every social conversation has to take place across a barbed wire fence of 'tolerance'.

Nowhere is this trend clearer than in India. There is a long history of applying heavy-handed censorship supposedly to ease fraught relationships between different communities, a process that in recent decades has greatly intensified. Hand in hand with more oppressive censorship has come, however, not a more peaceful society but one in which the sense of a common nation has increasingly broken down into sectarian rivalries, as every group demands its right not to be offended. The confrontation over *The Satanic Verses* was a classic example. In 1988, the authorities caved into Islamist pressure and banned Rushdie's novel. Not only did this embolden Muslims

to continue pushing for censorship, Rose suggests, but it encouraged other groups to follow suit. Hindus, he says, 'learnt from Muslims. Because the Indian government gave into the Muslims, the Hindus then came forward and said, "We also want to be accommodated in the same way. We want things we don't like banned." What it shows is that if you start to give in, there is no end to it.'

A week after I interviewed Rose, a train of events was set off that perfectly illustrated his observations. Salman Rushdie had been due to give a talk at the Jaipur Literature Festival about his Booker-winning novel *Midnight's Children*, the film of which is to be released later this year. Muslim activists issued threats. Instead of standing up to the bullies, both local and state governments caved in, exerting pressure on the festival organisers to keep Rushdie away. The organisers in turn surrendered, condemning four writers, Hari Kunzru, Amitava Kumar, Jeet Thayil and Rushir Joshi, all speakers at the festival who had shown solidarity with Rushdie by reading from *The Satanic Verses*. It was, they insisted, 'unnecessary provocation' and threatened that 'all necessary, consequential action' would be taken against any others who followed suit. Emboldened by this show of weakness, Muslim activists pushed further still, forcing organisers to abandon subsequent plans for Rushdie to talk to the festival by video link.

Next it was the turn of Hindus. A week after Islamists kept Rushdie out of Jaipur, Hindu activists forced Pune's Symbiosis University to cancel a screening of *Jashn-e-Azadi,* a new film about Kashmir, because it was 'anti-India', and to abandon a three-day seminar on the issue. If Muslims could suppress material they found obnoxious, the Hindu activists insisted, so could they.

And then, the following week, Sikhs picked up the baton. The American comedian Jay Leno had suggested that US Republican presidential hopeful Mitt Romney was so rich that he could hire the Golden Temple in Amritsar as his summer home. The Shiromani Gurdwara Parbandhak Committee, the so-called Sikh parliament in India, lodged a protest with the US ambassador to Delhi and called for worldwide protests against this insufferable insult. One Sikh filed a lawsuit against Leno in the American courts for 'exposing Sikhs and their religion to hatred, contempt, ridicule and obloquy'.

'If you set up a marketplace of outrage,' as the novelist Monica Ali has vividly observed, 'you have to expect everyone to enter it. Everyone now wants to say, "My feelings are more hurt than yours."' The demand that one should not give offence has created not a less conflicted world but one that has become more sectarian, fragmented and tribal.

Tolerance, in the way that Rose defines it, cannot, however, be a one-way street. If, as he insists, Muslims have to accept the right of others to blaspheme or cause offence, surely those others accept the right of Muslims (and of anyone else) to do the same? In reality, the opposite has happened. Hand in hand with the criminalising of criticism or ridicule of Islam has come the criminalising of Islamic dissent. Islamist preachers, such as Abu Hamza, whose incendiary sermons at Finsbury Park Mosque in north London were supposed to have influenced the 7/7 bombers, and Abu Izzadeen, who was filmed praising jihad as the 'responsibility of every single Muslim', have received long prison sentences for sermons deemed unacceptable. Most bizarre was the trial and conviction (subsequently overturned on appeal) of Samina Malik, a 23-year-old fantasist from West London who dreamed of jihad, and wrote awful poetry under the moniker of the 'Lyrical Terrorist', including such unforgettable lines as 'Let us make Jihad / Move to the front line / To chop chop head of kuffar swine.'

Rose accepts that at the time he first published the cartoons he would probably have argued for the imprisonment of Hamza, Izzadeen and Malik. What the cartoon controversy taught him, however, is that Muslims have as much right to offend, to abuse his beliefs, as he has to offend theirs. He has, as he says, 'definitely become a free speech fundamentalist'. So where would he now draw the line when it comes to freedom of expression? 'At incitement to violence,' Rose responds, but only 'incitement to violence in the First Amendment sense. There needs to be a clear and present danger that violence will follow words in a quite short time frame.'

In February 2006, around 300 Muslims gathered outside the Danish Embassy in London, protesting against the cartoons. Four of the protesters were imprisoned for between four and six years for shouting slogans such as 'Annihilate those who insult Islam,' 'Bomb, bomb Denmark. Bomb, bomb USA' and 'Europe, you will pay with your blood'. Had they committed a

1979 – Poland

The Gdansk Inter-Factory Strike Committee, which is to become the trade union Solidarity (Solidarność), demands freedom of expression as part of its 21 demands to the government, presented on 3 September. The Solidarity logo's trademark red and white becomes a symbol of resistance.

crime? No, says Rose. 'There was no clear and present danger that those words would be followed up by action.' The protesters, in other words, had been incarcerated not so much for bad acts as for bad thoughts.

The imprisoning of the radical preachers and the cartoon protesters has led to cries of 'Islamophobia'. Western governments, many claim, are deliberately targeting Muslims for possessing unacceptable thoughts. Yet many of those now crying 'foul' are the ones who have paved the way for such actions. It is true that over the past decade the war on terror has provided a pretext to impose greater restrictions on civil liberties. It would be wrong to pin the blame for such curtailment of free expression simply on 'Islamophobia'. The authorities have been able to curtail Islamic dissent by exploiting a culture of censorship that already existed, a culture created by the campaign against offensive, blasphemous and hateful speech. Western governments have seized upon the idea that it is wrong to give offence and transformed it into a weapon against radical Muslims as well as against critics of Islam. The moral of the story is that one should be careful what one wishes for. If we invite the state to define the boundaries of acceptable speech, we should not be surprised if it is not just speech to which we object that gets curtailed.

Critics of *Jyllands-Posten* retort that the cartoon controversy had little to do with free speech. It was simply about targeting Muslims. It is true that *Jyllands-Posten* is, as the critics suggest, a conservative paper, often hostile to immigration and obsessed by the threat of Islam. But that is an argument against its political stance, not against its right to publish cartoons that some may see as offensive or blasphemous. After all, it is not just those with nice liberal views who have the right to free speech; though increasingly many have come to believe that it should be.

More pertinent, perhaps, is the charge that, far from being a defender of free speech, *Jyllands-Posten* betrays double standards. In 2003, the newspaper had refused to publish cartoons about Jesus by the caricaturist Christoffer Zieler. 'I don't think *Jyllands-Posten*'s readers will enjoy the drawings,' the editor Carsten Juste wrote to Zieler. 'As a matter of fact, I think they will provoke an outcry.'

Rose dismisses the charge of double standards. The drawings, he told me, had actually been rejected because they had been 'of poor quality', but the editor 'had made the mistake of not telling the artist directly', instead 'rejecting his work with reference to the possible offence it might cause to the paper's readership'. *Jyllands-Posten* has, he says, often published cartoons offensive to Christians and Jews, including ones by Kurt Westergaard.

One Westergaard cartoon depicts Jesus on the cross with dollar signs in his eyes; another shows an undernourished Palestinian caught up in a barbed-wire fence in the shape of the Star of David. 'We were not specifically trying to offend Muslims rather than anyone else,' Rose insists.

Whatever one thinks of this defence – and I remain unconvinced – there is no denying the long history of liberal hypocrisy about free speech. John Milton, whose *Areopagitica*, his famous 1644 'speech for the liberty of unlicenc'd printing', is still rightly regarded as one of the great defences of free speech, opposed the extension of freedoms to Catholics. John Locke, upon whose work rests the philosophical foundations of liberalism, and whose *Letter Concerning Toleration* is a key text in the development of modern liberal ideas about freedom of expression and worship, similarly drew the line at extending freedom and liberties to Catholics and to atheists. 'No opinions contrary to human society, or to those moral rules which are necessary to the preservation of civil society,' he insisted, 'are to be tolerated.'

Double standards need to be confronted by extending speech

Many contemporary defenders of free speech would similarly draw the line at Muslims, often for many of the same reasons. From Geert Wilders' campaign to outlaw the Quran, to Ayaan Hirsi Ali's support for the Swiss ban on the building of minarets, to Martin Amis's 'thought experiment' on how 'the Muslim community will have to suffer until it gets its house in order', hypocrisy and double standards are rife in contemporary debates about freedom and liberties. Such double standards can, of course, work both ways. While some are reluctant to extend basic freedoms to Muslims, or hold Muslims to standards not demanded of non-Muslims, others on the contrary are happy to criticise or ridicule Christianity or conservatism or communism in a way that they would not dream of doing to Islam.

Double standards need to be confronted, not by extending restrictions but by extending speech, by ensuring not that everyone is equally deprived of liberties but that all are equally sheltered by them. To see how we should deal with double standards today, we only have to ask ourselves how we should have responded in the age of Milton and Locke. Should we have suggested that the best way to deal with their anti-Catholic bigotry was to extend to everyone the restrictions that Milton and Locke wished imposed on Catholics? Or should we have argued that restrictions on Catholics were wrong and that all deserved liberty? With four centuries worth of hindsight the answer to most people is crystal clear. It should be equally so today, in response to free speech and the hypocrisy of anti-Muslim prejudices.

Prejudice reveals itself not simply in double standards but also in a distorted image of the 'Other'. In the case of *Jyllands-Posten*, the newspaper used the publication of the cartoons to play upon tawdry stereotypes of Muslims, helping promote the idea that the views of radical Islamists represented that of all Muslims.

The publication of the cartoons caused no immediate reaction, even in Denmark. Only when journalists, disappointed by the lack of controversy, contacted a number of imams for their response did Islamists begin to recognise the opportunity provided not just by the caricatures themselves but also by the sensitivity of Danish society to their publication.

Among the first contacted was the controversial cleric Ahmed Abu Laban, infamous for his support for Osama bin Laden and the 9/11 attacks. He seized upon the cartoons to transform himself into a spokesman for Denmark's Muslims. His Islamic Society of Denmark was closely linked to the Muslim Brotherhood but had little support among Danish Muslims. Danish Muslims, as the sociologist Jytte Klausen points out, 'are for the most part politically placid and disinclined to support Islamic radicals and extremists'. But, observes Klausen in *The Cartoons that Shook the World*, her academic study of the controversy, *Jyllands-Posten*'s 'attack on the "mad mullahs" stereotyped all Danish Muslims as radical extremists'.

Rose acknowledges that this was exactly what happened. 'I think it was a mistake,' he says, 'a mistake not just made by *Jyllands-Posten* but a mistake broadly being made by the media, that every time you wanted to hear a Muslim voice, you went to one of these radical imams. That reinforced that sense of us versus them.'

The idea of a 'clash of civilisations' between Islam and the West, an idea first popularised by the American political scientist Samuel Huntington a decade before 9/11, has for many come to define the following decade. But it is not just conservatives, or those hostile to Islam, who have come to see the world in this way. Many of the fiercest critics of the 'clash of civilisations' thesis, many of *Jyllands-Posten*'s harshest opponents, have themselves helped promote the idea of a world divided into irreconcilable cultures.

There were many Danish Muslims who were happy to see the publication of the cartoons. Bunyamin Simsek was a councillor in the city of Aarhus. He was religious – he attends mosque, does not drink or eat pork and fasts at Ramadan. But he was also secular. 'There is,' he insisted, 'a large group of Muslims in this city who want to live in a secular society and adhere to the principle that religion is an issue between them and God and not something that should involve society.' Appalled by the way that Raed Hlayhel and Ahmed Abu Laban had come to be seen as the authentic spokesmen for Muslim concerns, Simsek set up a network of Muslims opposed to the Islamists and helped organise a counter demonstration to the cartoon protests. 'We wanted to show that not all Danish Muslims are Islamists,' he said. 'In fact very few are. But it is the Islamists like Raed Hlayhel and Abu Laban who get all the hearing.'

Voices such as Simsek's were rarely heard in the media because they did not fit into the narrative of what constituted a Muslim, a narrative promoted by liberals as well as conservatives, by those sympathetic to Islam as well as those hostile to the faith. The Danish MP Nasser Khader, like Simsek a critic of the campaign against the cartoons, tells of a conversation with Toger Seidenfaden, editor of *Politiken*, a left-wing newspaper highly critical of *Jyllands-Posten* and of the publication of the cartoons. 'He said to me that the cartoons insulted all Muslims,' Khader recalled. 'I said I was not insulted. He said, "But you're not a real Muslim."'

For left and right, for liberal and conservative, to be a proper Muslim was to be offended by the cartoons. Once Muslim authenticity is so defined, then only a figure such as Abu Laban can be seen as a true Muslim voice. Bunyamin Simsek and Nasser Khader – and Salman Rushdie – came to be regarded as too westernised, secular or progressive to be truly of their community. Because only one side of the conversation is regarded as 'authentic', what is often in reality a debate within the community which comes to be seen as offensive to the community itself. This is not just true of Muslims. The Sikh protesters who forced Gurpreet Kaur Bhatti's play *Behzti* offstage in 2004, a year before the cartoons were published, were seen as more authentically Sikh than Kaur Bhatti herself. And so have Jewish, Christian, Hindu and a host of other protesters who have in recent years cried 'Offence!' about films, plays, novels or art that they have disliked.

Both sides in this debate about Islam have hijacked the issue of free speech, bending and distorting the concept of liberty until it has become almost meaningless. On one side are those who ostensibly defend free speech, but do so only in tribal terms, as a weapon to be wielded by the

West against Islam, a means of depriving Muslims of basic liberties. On the other, are those who ostensibly defend liberties, and Muslims, but only by constraining free speech, incarcerating the very means by which we are able to think and debate and argue, and be human. Both sides are, in their different ways, enemies of free speech, of liberty, of our essential humanness. Seven years on from the cartoon crisis, two decades after the Rushdie affair, 40 years after the founding of *Index on Censorship*, our task today is not just to defend free speech but to liberate it from the shackles of bad faith. ❐

©Kenan Malik
41(1): 40/53
DOI: 10.1177/0306422012440233
www.indexoncensorship.org

Kenan Malik is the author of *From Fatwa to Jihad* (Atlantic) and a prolific commentator, broadcaster and writer

PACIFIC★STANDARD

Pacific Standard provides a unique perspective and insight into the social, political, and economic forces defining the world today. With an emphasis on fact-based, research-driven content; the magazine publishes fresh, compelling articles on the global economy, environmental issues, education, and health. *Pacific Standard* is essential reading for policymakers, thought leaders, and influential audiences interested in the latest innovation and ingenuity shaping research, industry, and global policy.

WORDS AND DEEDS

The post-war consensus on banning hate speech in Europe is based on an erroneous understanding of its role in the Holocaust, says **Flemming Rose**

Besides the issue of self-censorship, the debate ensuing from the cartoons revealed a number of fractures in European culture and self-understanding. One of these arose from the trauma of the Second World War, an event Europe at all costs wished to avoid repeating. The lesson learned from the Jewish Holocaust was that words could kill, and hateful words would beget hateful actions. It was widely held that if only the Weimar government had clamped down on the National Socialists' verbal persecution of the Jews in the years prior to Hitler's rise to power, or if the Nazis had been prevented from pursuing their propaganda of hatred following 1933, then the Holocaust would never have happened. Proponents of this view saw a parallel between unfettered freedom of speech, demonisation of the Jews in Nazi propaganda, and their subsequent extinction in the concentration camps. It was the same train of thought that prompted Denmark's former foreign minister,

Per Stig Møller, to warn in 2009 that free speech could be abused to incite violence. We see it today in the message being sent out by Osama bin Laden. And we saw it in Germany, where anti-Semitic rhetoric eventually led to *die Endlösung*, the Final Solution, by which six million Jews were killed,' he wrote in a newspaper article.

The assertion that Nazi propaganda had played a significant role in mobilising anti-Jewish sentiment is irrefutable. But to claim that the Holocaust could have been prevented if only anti-Semitic speech and Nazi propaganda had been banned was to stretch a point. Anti-Semitism in the Weimar Republic sparking off violence and calls for Jews to be deprived of all rights was one thing. Another was Nazi apartheid, the exclusion of Jews from German society under Hitler in the 1930s, the annulment of Jewish civil rights, the *Kristallnacht*, or Night of Broken Glass, and the pogroms. Still another was the Holocaust. What unites them, however, is that at no point did freedom of speech exist unhindered in Germany in the period in question.

In the wake of the Holocaust, European democracies concluded that a ban on hate speech could prevent, or at least contain, racist violence and killings. The Allies duly enforced legislation to that effect on Germany and Austria in the immediate aftermath of war, believing it to be insurance against a repeat Holocaust. History, however, provided no evidence by which to legitimise such reasoning. Nonetheless, it was a logic that formed the basis of international efforts towards the protection of human rights in the post-war decades. Jewish organisations also played an active role in the process. Presumably, they had little idea of how far it would lead.

The ball began rolling with the UN International Covenant on Civil and Political Rights in 1965, which entered into force a year later, and the UN Convention on Racial Discrimination of 1965, which took effect in 1969. Committees were set up by the UN to monitor the extent to which member states upheld the conventions. A couple of decades previously, following its inception in 1949, the Council of Europe had taken steps towards establishing the European Convention for the Protection of Human Rights, the world's first human rights treaty, taking effect in 1953. The European Court of Human Rights was encharged by the Council of Europe with monitoring and dealing with complaints by citizens who believed their rights according to the Convention to have been violated within a member state. In 1998, the institution was made permanent. The number of members of the Council of Europe grew in the wake of the Cold War to 47 countries. A commensurate rise occurred in the number of complaints to the Court: from 138 in 1955, the figure sky-rocketed to some 41,000 in 2005. The Court was not a court of appeal. It was not empowered to nullify the ruling of courts of law at the national level, but it could order a member state to align its practice with the Convention in the case that it ruled in favour of a plaintiff.

This was a quite momentous and indeed laudable development. For the first time, individuals were accorded global rights transgressing national boundaries. After the millennium, however, the constraints on free speech enforced by the conventions on national legislations were to become a significant instrument for grievance fundamentalists and for authoritarian regimes which made use of them to justify oppression of alternative thinkers and of ethnic and religious minorities. This tended to occur with particular reference to two articles: Article 20, paragraph 2 of the Covenant on Civil and Political Rights, and Article 4 of the Convention on the Elimination of All Forms of Racial Discrimination.

The first of these runs as follows: 'Any advocacy of national, racial or religious hatred that constitutes incitement to discrimination, hostility or violence shall be prohibited by law.' The second, taking as its point of departure a rather broad definition of racial discrimination, declared that the state: 'Shall declare an offence punishable by law all dissemination of ideas based on racial superiority or hatred, incitement to racial discrimination [. . .] against any race or group of persons of another colour or ethnic origin.' Moreover, states were obliged to prohibit organisations and propaganda activities promoting or inciting racial discrimination, just as participation in such organisations or activities was to be made punishable by law.

The wording was awkward and technical, though the intention was clear: words and actions were to be considered parallel. There was to be no principle difference between saying something discriminatory and performing discriminatory actions. With time, definitions of racism and discrimination widened, the distinction between words and actions becoming commensurately more blurred. With a public sector growing by the year, the welfare state was afforded wide-reaching privileges

and the responsibility of ensuring a new form of equality among citizens. Individuals were no longer simply to enjoy equal opportunities, but were to be ensured equal results. In the welfare state, there were to be no differences, and the rights of the individual were to give way to those of the community.

Things came to a head with immigration to Europe from the Islamic world in particular. European welfare states suddenly found themselves under pressure. The new diversity, the gaps that emerged in cultures and religions and ways of living meant on the one hand that the welfare state had to impose demands on its new citizens to make them adapt to the norms of the society and thereby ensure a continued community of values. On the other hand, the welfare state was forced to take measures against those of its indigenous citizens who expressed discontent with these new demographic developments and who did so in a language it considered to be a threat to social stability and the right not to be subjected to utterances of a discriminatory nature. Wide-reaching freedom of speech essentially ran against the grain of the ideology of the welfare state in a multicultural society.

The grievance lobby in the UN, the EU and the human rights industry was directed by a notion that criminalisation of racist utterances, so-called hate speech, would lead to racism being eradicated. They drew up a succession of reports urging member states to prosecute and sentence perpetrators of hate speech to a much greater degree than before. The grievance lobby wanted the definition of racism expanded so as to encompass still more groups within society. Their whole perspective was driven by the notion of insult: theirs was a world all about identifying the victims of freedom of speech and those guilty of its abuse. Those who defended the offended could adorn themselves with the halos of justice. If they who offended were found guilty and punished, a good deed had been done for a better world.

The modern dispute as to the boundaries of free speech began with the Nuremberg trials of 1945-46 in which 24 Nazis stood accused for their roles in the genocide of the Second World War. The trials established that there were clear ties between the Nazis' mobilisation of the media, which in words and pictures had demonised and blackened the character of the Jews, and the subsequent Holocaust. Julius Streicher, former editor of the anti-Semitic tabloid *Der Stürmer*, was among those the tribunal condemned to death. During the process, Streicher was singled out as 'Jew-Baiter Number One'. The judgment against him ran:

'In his speeches and articles, week after week, month after month, he infected the German mind with the virus of anti-Semitism and incited the German people to active persecution [. . .] Streicher's incitement to murder and extermination at the time when Jews in the East were being killed under the most horrible conditions clearly constitutes persecution on political and racial grounds in connection with war crimes as defined by the Charter, and constitutes a crime against humanity.'

This take on the genesis of the Holocaust formed the basis of an understanding of the relationship between words and actions that led increasingly to the outlawing of verbal affront. What was ignored in such cases, however, was the fact that Streicher's and other Nazis' Jew-baiting occurred in a society utterly devoid of freedom of speech: under Hitler, no freedom existed by which to counter the witch-hunt against the Jewish community. Germany was ruled by a tyranny of silence.

The premise came out of an idea characterising totalitarian societies laid out in George Orwell's masterful novel *1984*. The verbal hygiene of the totalitarian state was to ensure the development of the ideal society. Words established what they denoted; banning mention of entities and phenomena meant they would cease to exist. Thus, language became an instrument for creating the world in one's own image: war is peace, freedom is slavery, ignorance is strength.

In the Soviet Union, the machinery of propaganda vanished away nationalism; ethnic and religious tensions – with the exception of isolated, post-capitalist pockets that would soon be swallowed up by communism – were likewise non-existent. In books and films, art and the media, the magic eraser of the censor wiped out whatever didn't fit the Marxist-Leninist version of reality. Party Secretary Mikhail Gorbachev believed so devoutly in the orally hygienic, beautified image that at first he was unable to grasp what was happening as national separatist movements rose up to eventually condemn the Soviet Union to history's dump. The notion that social evils could be eradicated by prohibiting certain kinds of utterance was completely in tune with the self-image of Soviet ideology. In a dictatorship, no principle distinction exists between words and actions.

The claim that the Holocaust was the result of Nazi 'abuse of freedom of speech' failed to distinguish between the totalitarian society, in which no freedoms existed by which to counter, ridicule and expose racist propaganda, and, by contrast, the open, democratic society whose citizens were at liberty to say whatever they wanted to uncover the lies of National Socialism, a society in which the public space was an open market of competing ideas and in which intimidation of individuals and groups within society never went unchallenged.

In Weimar Germany, insulting communities of faith – Protestant, Catholic or Jew – was a punishable offence commanding up to three years' imprisonment. Similarly, the dissemination of false rumour with the intention of degrading or showing contempt for other individuals could result in two years. Incitement to class warfare or acts of violence towards other social classes was also prohibited by law, likewise punishable by up to two years behind bars. It was a piece of legislation to which the Jewish community often sought recourse in order to defend themselves against anti-Semitic attacks. Anti-Semites countered, occasionally with success, by claiming their attacks on Jews were not incitement to class hatred, but were instead aimed at the Jewish 'race' and therefore not an offence.

The notion that freedom of speech was unconstrained in Weimar Germany was a fallacy. The reality of the matter was that political violence flourished without intervention by the authorities. Leading Nazis such as Joseph Goebbels, Theodor Fritsch and Julius Streicher were all prosecuted for their anti-Semitic utterances. Streicher served two prison sentences. Rather than deterring the Nazis and preventing anti-Semitism, the many court cases served as effective public relations machinery for Streicher's efforts, affording him the kind of attention he never would have found had his racist utterances been made in a climate of free and open debate. Only weeks after Streicher was sentenced to two months imprisonment for anti-Semitism, the Nazis trebled their share of the vote at the state legislature election in Thuringia. One of the charges brought against Streicher and his associate, Karl Holz, concerned *Der Stürmer* having construed a number of unsolved murders as ritual killings perpetrated by Jews. The second concerned claims published in the paper that the Jewish faith permitted perjury before non-Jewish courts.

Bernhard Weiss, Vice-President of the Berlin police, regularly dragged Goebbels into court on charges of anti-Semitism. In all these cases brought against the future head of Nazi propaganda, the prosecution came out on top, yet according to one observer, in the public eye Weiss consistently ended up looking more like the loser, as Goebbels' anti-Semitic invective found a platform in the public process.

'The Vice-President of police may have been better served by simply allowing the Nazi attacks to echo away in silence,' mused Dietz Bering in an anthology on the Jews of the Weimar Republic.

In April 1932, Nazis plastered the city of Nuremberg with posters proclaiming *Die Juden sind unser Unglück!* (The Jews are our misfortune). It was the motto of *Der Stürmer*.

To begin with, police refused to remove them, despite a formal complaint being lodged by the Jewish Central Committee. The argument was that the posters could not be considered an incitement to violence, but when the Central Committee went to the authorities in Munich the posters were removed. In October of the same year, a young non-Jewish girl in the northern part of the country died when her Jewish boyfriend tried to help her perform an abortion. The young man tried to get rid of the body by cutting it into pieces and scattering them over a wide rural area. For *Der Stürmer*, it was a case made in heaven, but when the paper appeared with a detailed description of the events construed as a Jewish ritual murder, the issue was confiscated and the editor responsible later convicted of causing religious affront.

In the period 1923 to 1933, *Der Stürmer* was either confiscated or its editors taken to court on no fewer than 36 separate occasions. In 1928, the paper and its staff were the subjects of five litigations in the space of 11 days. Proceedings, however, gave the general public the impression that Streicher was more significant than was the case. Those instances where Streicher was sentenced to terms of imprisonment were a golden opportunity for him to portray himself as a victim and martyr. The more charges he faced, the greater became the admiration of his supporters. On the occasions on which he was sent to jail, Streicher was accompanied on his way by hundreds of sympathisers in what looked like his triumphal entry into martyrdom. In 1930, he was greeted by thousands of fans outside the prison, among them Hitler himself. The German courts became an important platform for Streicher's campaign against the Jews. Some observers suggested that the cases brought against him prompted critics of the Nazis to relax complacently in the faith that the judicial system alone was capable of combating National Socialism.

According to historian Dennis E Showalter, author of a book about Streicher and *Der Stürmer* during the Weimar Republic, the judicial system found itself ill-equipped to stem the tide of anti-Semitism, though its shortcomings were by no means attributable to a lack of legislation or Nazi bias. 'The familiar cliché that Weimar's legal system was not particularly interested in protecting Jews, and avoided doing so when it could, requires significant revision [. . .] The regional legal system included active and potential Nazi sympathisers. Yet in general, the courts of northern Bavaria sustained the Jewish legal position even in one of Nazism's strongholds,' Showalter stated.

In the view of Alan Borovoy, general counsel of the Canadian Civil Liberties Association (CCLA), in the Weimar Republic in the time leading up to Hitler's claiming power in 1933,

cases were regularly brought against individuals on account of anti-Semitic speech. 'Remarkably, pre-Hitler Germany had laws very much like the Canadian anti-hate law. Moreover, those laws were enforced with some vigour. During the 15 years before Hitler came to power, there were more than 200 prosecutions based on anti-Semitic speech [. . .] As subsequent history so painfully testifies, this type of legislation proved ineffectual on the one occasion when there was a real argument for it,' Bovory writes in his 1988 book *When Freedoms Collide: The Case for Civil Liberties*.

The widely made claim that hate speech against the Jews was a primary factor of the Holocaust has no empirical support. In fact, one might forcefully argue that what paved the way for Holocaust was the *ban* on hate speech, in so far as it handed Streicher and other Nazis a glorious opportunity to bait the Jewish community in the German courtrooms and in a national press, which otherwise would have spared them precious little ink. For the democrats of the Weimar Republic, a far more effective strategy would have been to address Nazi propaganda in free and open public debate, but in Europe between the wars confidence in free speech was running low. ❐

©Flemming Rose

This is an edited extract from Flemming Rose's book *The Tyranny of Silence*. It is its first publication in English.

Index supporter Kurt Vonnegut writes for the magazine in 1981 (next page)

[top portion of page illegible/blurred]

I gather from what I read in the papers and hear on television that you imagine me, and some other writers, too, as being sort of ratlike people who enjoy making money from poisoning the minds of young people. I am in fact a large, strong person, fifty-one years old, who did a lot of farm work as a boy, who is good with tools. I have raised six children, three my own and three adopted. They have all turned out well. Two of them are farmers. I am a combat infantry veteran from World War II, and hold a Purple Heart. I have earned whatever I own by hard work. I have

[right column top partially illegible]

If you were to bother to read my books, to behave as educated persons would, you would learn that they are not sexy, and do not argue in favour of wildness of any kind. They beg that people be kinder and more responsible than they often are. It is true that some of the characters speak coarsely. That is because people speak coarsely in real life. Especially soldiers and hardworking men speak coarsely, and even our most sheltered children know that. And we all know, too, that those words really don't damage children much. They didn't damage us when we were young. It was evil deeds and lying that hurt us.

After I have said all this, I am sure you are still ready to respond, in effect, 'Yes, yes — but it still remains our right and our responsibility to decide what books our children are going to be made to read in our community.' This is surely so. But it is also true that if you exercise that right and fulfil that responsibility in an ignorant, harsh, un-American manner, then people are entitled to call you bad citizens and fools. Even your own children are entitled to

Literature as encouragement

I doubt that literature has ever triumphed over repression. I think of Hitler in his bunker, with a pistol at his temple and with the Red Army only a few blocks away, and I have to admit that the overthrow of a tyrant is not a literary enterprise.

Literature has, however, encouraged some repressed people to behave as proudly and honourably and humanely as possible, under the circumstances, and it has suggested to them models for a better society and better citizens, should the tyranny be overthrown. The American Revolutionary War comes to mind. The powers of a monarchy were repudiated, and a Declaration of Independence and a Constitution were written by a few highly literate men, and the ideas in these documents were drawn, directly or indirectly, from nearly the whole of Western literature.

Literature will always be at cross-purposes with autocrats. This is not because authors have always been enthusiasts for freedom. It is because authors, if they are to find willing readers, must depict human beings as somehow marvellous, as enchanting observers and reasoners and makers of important decisions on their own. Autocrats, on the other hand, would prefer their subjects to have low opinions of themselves and their neighbours, to consider human beings unworthy of justice and dignity and privacy and independent thinking and so on. Literature, in order to be interesting, has always tended to weaken self-loathing — even in prisons and lunatic asylums and military installations — simply everywhere.

This means trouble.   **Kurt Vonnegut**

JUMP 2

RISE TO THE CHALLENGE OF WRITING AND SUSTAINING YOUR CREATIVE PROCESS

Let a team of professional writers take you out of your creative comfort zone. Find out how to overcome hurdles and set-backs, manage your time effectively and learn coaching tools to help you realise your writing goals.

SUNDAY 25 MARCH, 10AM – 4.30PM

Free Word Centre, 60 Farringdon Road, London, EC1R 3GA

Choose 2 out of 3 workshops from each session

Morning

WRITE WHAT YOU DON'T KNOW
with Clare Pollard
Be liberated by taking a plunge into the unknown.

OBJECT LESSONS
with Imogen Robertson
Find inspiration for new characters and plot lines.

NOT JUST SITTIN' AND CHATTIN'
with Ola Animashawun
Create dialogue that leaps off the page or lights up the stage.

Afternoon

FINDING THE RIGHT PUBLISHER
with Juliette Mitchell
Advice on publishers, agents and pitching your work.

SUSTAINING THE CREATIVE PROCESS
with Shaun Levin
How to integrate writing into all aspects of your life.

JUMP-ING! WHAT'S STOPPING YOU?
with Gaylene Gould
Learn coaching techniques to further your writing.

£55/£45 concessions
For more information or to book:
www.spreadtheword.org.uk or phone 020 7735 3111

spread the word looking out for London's writers   FREE**WORD**

My first memories of censorship are cinematic: screen kisses brutalised by prudish scissors which chopped out the moments of actual contact. (Briefly, before comprehension dawned, I wondered if that were all there was to kissing, the languorous approach and then the sudden turkey-jerk away.) The effect was usually somewhat comic, and censorship still retains, in contemporary Pakistan, a strong element of comedy. When the Pakistani censors found that the movie *El Cid* ended with a dead Charlton Heston leading the Christians to victory over live Moslems, they nearly banned it until they had the idea of simply cutting out the entire climax, so that the film as screened showed El Cid mortally wounded, El Cid dying nobly, and then it ended. Moslems 1, Christians 0.

The comedy is sometimes black. The burning of the film *Kissa Kursi Ka* ('Tale of a Chair') during Mrs Gandhi's Emergency rule in India is notorious; and, in Pakistan, a reader's letter to the *Pakistan Times*, in support of the decision to ban the film *Gandhi* because of its unflattering portrayal of M A Jinnah, criticised certain 'liberal elements' for having dared to suggest that the film should be released so that Pakistanis could make up their own minds about it. If they were less broad-minded, the letter-writer suggested, these persons would be better citizens of Pakistan.

My first direct encounter with censorship took place in 1968, when I was 21, fresh out of Cambridge and full of the radical fervour

OPINION

Last chance?
Salman Rushdie

of that famous year. I returned to Karachi where a small magazine commissioned me to write a piece about my impressions on returning home. I remember very little about this piece (mercifully, memory is a censor, too), except that it was not at all political. It tended, I think, to linger melodramatically on images of dying horses with flies settling on their eyeballs. You can imagine the sort of thing. Anyway, I submitted my piece, and a couple of weeks later was told by the magazine's editor that the Press Council, the national censors, had banned it completely. Now it so happened that I had an uncle on the Press Council, and in a very unradical, string-pulling mood I thought I'd just go and see him and everything would be sorted out. He looked tired when I confronted him. 'Publication,' he said immovably, 'would not be in your best interests.' I never found out why.

Next I persuaded Karachi TV to let me produce and act in Edward Albee's *The Zoo Story*, which they liked because it was 45 minutes long, had a cast of two and required only a park bench for a set. I then had to go through a series of astonishing censorship conferences. The character I played had a long monologue in which he described his landlady's dog's repeated attacks on him. In an attempt to befriend the dog, he bought it half a dozen hamburgers. The dog refused the hamburgers and attacked him again. 'I was offended.' I was supposed to say. 'It was six perfectly good hamburgers with not enough pork in them to make it disgusting.' 'Pork,' a TV executive told me solemnly, 'is a four-letter word.' He had said the same thing about 'sex' and 'homosexual.' But this time I argued back. The text, I pleaded, was saying the right thing about pork. Pork, in Albee's view, made hamburgers so disgusting that even dogs refused them. This was superb anti-pork propaganda. It must stay. 'You don't see,' the executive told me, wearily. 'the same word represented as an awful fact. Our moral pork may not be spoken on Pakistani television. And that was that. I also had to cut the description of being a substitute parent who tempt schoolboys and plants his seminars ...

do they contr... too. At the ... Aligned Mo... Pakistan pre... fearfulness. ... one of the ot... when they ... instance, or ... Hindus, or ... acts. Indian... depressed by ... numbers beh... moment and ...

What are ... Obviously, th... the presence ... campaign of ... news media ... Baluchistan v... died unoffic... comforted th... truth declare... example: you... of Pakistan"... booming here... the country's... underlies Gen... of the Afgha... enterprise th... business, and ... to make sure ... as well as th... the Quran do... the ethics of ...

But the w... censorship is ... the imaginatio... is no deba... remembering, ... suppressed ... becomes also... what the sug... becomes easy... suppressed t... dangerous th... And then th... The anti-Gan... needed some... virtue is our ... novel *Big Bro...*

It seems tha... conceived. I n... this release? ... Pakistan? ... the mumbo-ju... In 2 then a ...

LAST CHANCE?

Censorship in Pakistan has ranged from the ridiculous to the downright terrifying. But as the country entered a new phase, **Salman Rushdie** hoped for change

My first memories of censorship are cinematic: screen kisses brutalised by prudish scissors which chopped out the moments of actual contact. (Briefly, before comprehension dawned, I wondered if that were all there was to kissing, the languorous approach and then the sudden turkey-jerk away.) The effect was usually somewhat comic, and censorship still retains, in contemporary Pakistan, a strong element of comedy. When the Pakistani censors found that the movie El Cid ended with a dead Charlton Heston leading the Christians to victory over live Moslems, they nearly banned it until they had the idea of simply cutting out the entire climax, so that the film as screened showed El Cid mortally wounded. El Cid dying nobly, and then it ended. Muslims 1, Christians 0.

The comedy is sometimes black. The burning of the film *Kissa Kursi Ka* [Tale of a Chair] during Mrs Gandhi's Emergency rule in India is notorious; and, in Pakistan, a reader's letter to the *Pakistan Times*, in support of the decision to ban the film *Gandhi* because of its unflattering portrayal of MA Jinnah, criticised certain 'liberal elements' for having dared to suggest that the film should be released so that Pakistanis could make up their own minds about it. If they were less broad-minded, the letter writer suggested, these persons would be better citizens of Pakistan.

My first direct encounter with censorship took place in 1968, when I was 21, fresh out of Cambridge and full of the radical fervour of that famous year. I returned to Karachi where a small magazine commissioned me to write a piece about my impressions on returning home. I remember very little about this piece (mercifully, memory is a censor, too), except that it was not at all political. It tended, I think, to linger melodramatically on images of dying horses with flies settling on their eyeballs. You can imagine the sort of thing. Anyway, I submitted my piece, and a couple of weeks later was told by the magazine's editor that the Press Council, the national censors, had banned it completely. Now it so happened that I had an uncle on the Press Council, and in a very unradical, string-pulling mood I thought I'd

El Cid with Charlton Heston, 1961
Credit: SNAP/Rex Features

just go and see him and everything would be sorted out. He looked tired when I confronted him. 'Publication,' he said immovably, 'would not be in your best interests.' I never found out why.

Next I persuaded Karachi TV to let me produce and act in Edward Albee's *The Zoo Story*, which they liked because it was 45 minutes long, had a cast of two and required only a park bench for a set. I then had to go through a series of astonishing censorship conferences. The character I played had a long monologue in which he described his landlady's dog's repeated attacks on him. In an attempt to befriend the dog, he bought it half a dozen hamburgers. The dog refused the hamburgers and attacked him again. 'I was offended,' I was supposed to say. 'It was six perfectly good hamburgers with not enough pork in them to make it disgusting.'

'Pork', a TV executive told me solemnly, 'is a four-letter word.' He had said the same thing about 'sex', and 'homosexual', but this time I argued back. The text, I pleaded, was saying the right thing about pork. Pork, in Albee's view, made hamburgers so disgusting that even dogs refused them. This was superb anti-pork propaganda. It must stay. 'You don't see', the executive told me, wearing the same tired expression as my uncle had, 'the word pork may not be spoken on Pakistan television.' And that was that. I also had to cut the line about God being a coloured queen who wears a kimono and plucks his eyebrows.

The point I'm making is not that censorship is a source of amusement, which it usually isn't, but that – in Pakistan, at any rate – it is everywhere, inescapable, permitting no appeal. In India the authorities control the media that matter – radio and television – and allow some leeway to the press, comforted by their knowledge of the country's low literacy level. In Pakistan they go further. Not only do they control the press, but the journalists too. At the recent conference of the Non-Aligned Movement in New Delhi, the Pakistan press corps was notable for its fearfulness. Each member was worried that one of the other guys might inform on him when they returned – for drinking, for instance, or consorting too closely with Hindus, or performing other unpatriotic acts. Indian journalists were deeply depressed by the sight of their opposite numbers behaving like scared rabbits one moment and quislings the next.

What are the effects of total censorship? Obviously, the absence of information and the presence of lies. During Mr Bhutto's campaign of genocide in Balochistan, the news media remained silent. Officially, Balochistan was at peace. Those who died, died unofficial deaths. It must have comforted them to know that the State's truth declared them all to be alive. Another example: you will not find the involvement of Pakistan's military rulers with the booming heroin industry much discussed in the country's news media. Yet this is what underlies General Zia's concern for the lot of the Afghan refugees. It is Afghan free enterprise that runs the Pakistan heroin business, and they have had the good sense to make sure that they make the Army rich as well as themselves. How fortunate that the Quran does not mention anything about the ethics of heroin pushing.

But the worst, most insidious effect of censorship is that, in the end, it can deaden the imagination of the people. Where there is no debate, it is hard to go on remembering, every day, that there is a suppressed side to every argument. It becomes almost impossible to conceive of what the suppressed things might be. It becomes easy to think that what has been suppressed was valueless, anyway, or so dangerous that it needed to be suppressed. And then the victory of the censor is total. The anti-Gandhi letter writer who recommended narrow-mindedness as a national virtue is one such casualty of censorship; he loves Big Brother – or *Burra Bhai*, perhaps.

It seems, now, that General Zia's days are numbered. I do not believe that the present disturbances are the end, but they are the beginning of the end, because they show that the people have lost their fear of his brutal regime, and if the people cease to be afraid, he is done for. But Pakistan's big test will come after the end of dictatorship, after the restoration of civilian rule and free elections, whenever that is, in one year or two or five; because if leaders do not then emerge who are willing to lift censorship, to permit dissent, to believe and to demonstrate that opposition is the bedrock of democracy, then, I am afraid, the last chance will have been lost. For the moment, however, one can hope. ❒

©Salman Rushdie
41(1): 64/68
DOI: 10.1177/0306422012438656
www.indexoncensorship.org

Salman Rushdie's latest novel is *Luka and the Fire of Life* (Random House).This article was first published in *Index on Censorship* Volume 12, Number 6, December 1983

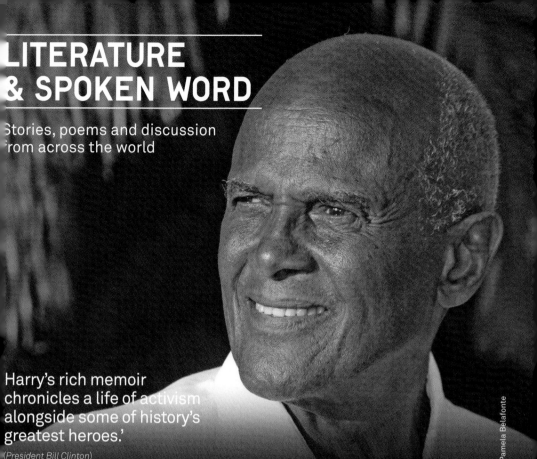

LITERATURE & SPOKEN WORD

Stories, poems and discussion from across the world

'Harry's rich memoir chronicles a life of activism alongside some of history's greatest heroes.'
(President Bill Clinton)

© Pamela Belafonte

'ESS GALLAGHER, JOHN KINSELLA, EAN SPRACKLAND & DOUGLAS DUNN
'uesday 20 March
Hear four outstanding poets from across the world read from and discuss their work.

CHIBUNDU ONUZO & NOO SARO-WIWA
'hursday 22 March
Two writers explore their native land of Nigeria through travelogue and fiction.

MAHFUZ MIR ALI, ROWYDA AMIN, NICK MAKOHA & SHAZEA QURAISHI
'hursday 29 March
Four poets read from their latest work in this special event to celebrate the *TEN* anthology.

'Sparkling new talents' *(Carol Ann Duffy)*

TICKETS 0844 847 9910
SOUTHBANKCENTRE.CO.UK

ALI BADER, INAAM KACHACHI & SAMUEL SHIMON
Monday 2 April
Three Iraqi authors take the pulse of their nation through new fiction.

ANNIE BAOBEI, LI ER & FENG TANG
Monday 16 April
An evening of short readings and music that catches the wave of contemporary Chinese culture.

JUNG CHANG
WILD SWANS 21 YEARS ON
Tuesday 24 April
Still banned in China, *Wild Swans* is the most successful non-fiction book in the UK. Jung Chang discusses the book, her subsequent writing and Chinese politics today.

HARRY BELAFONTE
Wednesday 6 June
Join us for an evening in conversation with a legend. Singer and activist Harry Belafonte talks about his involvement in the Civil Rights movement and his extraordinary life.

Supported by
ARTS COUNCIL ENGLAND

SOUTHBANK CENTRE

NEWS CHARADE

Kamila Shamsie

Pakistan is a country in the paradoxical position of having one of the most outspoken and powerful media in the world while being one of the world's deadliest countries for journalists. On the face of it, this may not appear paradoxical – surely it is precisely the outspokenness of the media that makes it so threatening and therefore a target. In fact, it is the selective self-censorship of most of the press which leaves individual journalists exposed when they step outside the rules of what can and can't be freely discussed. Doing away with that self-censorship is the most urgent concern in the battle for free expression.

The influence of the press can be noted in the fact that prime time TV in Pakistan is not composed of reality shows or comedies or thrillers, but political talk shows – which sometimes appear a mix of all of the above. When the most powerful talk show hosts speak, the nation listens. The man who has most cause to know the influence of the media is General Musharraf, whose fall from power is directly linked to the campaign waged against him by news channels, in tandem with lawyers seeking the restoration of the chief justice.

But even in the heady days when a free press stood up to a dictator, there was a limit to how far it was willing to go. Musharraf must go, elections must be held – but little was said of the all-pervasive role of the army and intelligence agencies in Pakistan. In a country too often obsessed with outward appearance it was ultimately cosmetic rather than structural changes the press asked for. So today, while civilian politicians are pilloried in the press, there is relative silence on the role of the army and intelligence agencies (with the exception of a few, brave journalists). Given that military intervention into political life is so entrenched, and every few months there are rumours of a fresh military coup, it does democracy no favours to turn a blind eye to the people who are really responsible for much of the mess in which Pakistan finds itself.

Nowhere is self-censorship of the press more notable than in the case of Balochistan, the most politically and economically marginalised province in the country, and a quagmire of competing interests. It is in Balochistan that most American drone attacks take place, in Balochistan that the Quetta Shura (composed of top leadership of the Afghan Taliban, with rumoured links to the ISI, Pakistan intelligence) is based, and in Balochistan that separatists have been waging a war against the central government, on and off, for decades. Yet very little news ever comes out of Balochistan, even while a large percentage of the journalists who are killed in Pakistan are reporting from there. These journalists are almost always local to the area – reporters from outside rarely venture there. Admittedly, this is almost entirely because of army restrictions – the military keeps the press out on the grounds that it's conducting sensitive military operations there (an ongoing situation for years). But where is the press's attempt to fight back against this?

A press which can take down a dictator can certainly unite to try and reverse the army's policy on the media in Balochistan – or find ways to give citizen journalists from the province prominence in media outlets. Instead what we have is a news blackout, while Baloch journalists, political activists, students and lawyers are 'disappeared' or tortured or killed.

Changing this will take courage, of course. The murdered journalists are testimony to the danger. But a press that prides itself on its power and independence only shames itself if it allows members of its tribe to be isolated and targeted. The refusal of an extremely powerful press to discuss the wall of silence around Balochistan is what makes the silence self-censorship. Tucking stories away at the bottom of news reports or the inside pages, on those rare instances when it's mentioned at all, makes things even worse – it allows the charade of pretending that there is no news blackout. But there is, and the media has allowed itself to be entirely complicit. ❐

©Kamila Shamsie
41(1):70/71
DOI: 10.1177/0306422012439380
www.indexoncensorship.org

Kamila Shamsie's most recent novel, *Burnt Shadows* (Bloomsbury), was shortlisted for the Orange Prize. She is a member of *Index*'s advisory board

THE ART OF CENSORSHIP

Magnum photographer **Abbas** laments an increasing culture of silence in Iran

Iranians live with censorship the way ancient Egyptians lived with the ten plagues: attacks come one after another, in great variety; they bring havoc and everyone does his best to avoid them.

Censorship corrupts all walks of life in Iran: politics and journalism, the internet and the cinema, visual arts and literature, dress code and women's voices – even children's stories. Journalists working for the western media are routinely asked by the secret police about their sources and requested not to write or broadcast unfavourable stories about Iran.

Sometimes censorship is the first step towards prison: when the Green Movement was mercilessly suppressed in 2009, journalist and documentary film director Maziar Bahari was arrested and underwent physical and psychological torture. He was freed after four months, thanks to an international campaign (read Maziar Bahari's manifesto on pp.80–81).

Officially it is not compulsory for a film, a novel, a play or a visual art exhibition to pass through the censor before creation or publication. The system is more hypocritical: censorship takes place afterwards. Thus a film or a novel can be banned or an exhibition taken off the walls after considerable sums of money have been invested.

For probing the boundaries of censorship, film director Jafar Panahi was handed down a six-year jail sentence – suspended so far – and a 20-year ban on making or directing any movies, writing screenplays and giving any form of interview to Iranian or foreign media, as well being prohibited from leaving the country. For having appeared in a western film, Ridley Scott's *Body of Lies*, actress Golshifteh Farahani has to live in exile in Paris.

There are two kinds of censorship in Iran: official, as in the cases above, and a more pernicious kind, where the same level of control and the same result can be achieved by making everyone a censor, by planting the idea of censorship in every Iranian's mind. This way, there is no need to employ large numbers of official censors. This brand of censorship has developed into an art form.

Iranians have also developed their response into an art form. Instead of confronting the censor, they bypass him.

Women are not allowed to sing and dance in public? Cultural evenings are organised in private homes where women play instruments, sing and dance!

The female nude is not to be displayed in galleries? Exhibitions are held in artists' studios!

A woman's hair is not to be shown outside her home? A photographer uses models who have no hair whatsoever as a result of a genetic condition!

An army of censors, most of them wounded veterans from the war with Iraq, dutifully apply dark ink to foreign magazines imported into Iran in order

to cover up all exposed parts of the female body? A photographer creates works of art using the same technique!

A woman's curves are not to be displayed? Fashion designers envelope the female body in beautiful loose patterns.

Censorship is self-defeating: without the restrictions imposed by the censor, would Iranian cinema have enjoyed the international success it does? Would Iranian art, including photography, be so alive? In a country under the tyranny of censorship, art becomes a struggle.

A great writer told me the best story about censorship. Mullahs, many of whom have graduated from Qom seminaries, are responsible for censoring books. But reading books all day broadens the horizons of the censor. So the mullahs become more lax in their censorship as time passes and have to be replaced every six months.

There is a price to pay though: Iran is a country of schizophrenic citizens, torn between censorship imposed in public life and the freedom they enjoy in the secrecy of their minds and homes. ❐

Captions

All photos © Abbas/Magnum

Page 72: Painters in Tehran, 2003

Pages 74–75: Azadeh Akhlagui photographs models wearing chadors. Both models are hairless due to a genetic condition

Page 76: Photographer Shadi Ghadirian at work on a series about censorship, 2005.

Documentary film director Maziar Bahari (right) and director of photography Mohammad Ahmadi scout a location for a film on Aids, 2003

Page 77: A woman poses for a portrait, Djamshidie Park, Tehran, 2000

Page 78: Actress Golshifte Farahani (right) and Maryam Mehrjui on location for an art video featuring Mehrjui and directed by her mother, Faryar Javaherian, November 2006

Jafaar Panahi (third from right, standing) directs Offside, a film about a girl who must dress like a boy to attend football matches, Tehran, June 2005

©Abbas
41(1): 72/79
DOI: 10.1177/0306422012438471
www.indexoncensorship.org

Abbas was born in Iran and lives in Paris. His photography has taken him all over the world, including Vietnam, Northern Ireland and Biafra. His latest book is *Les Enfants du lotus* (Editions de la Martinière)

BOILING POINT

Maziar Bahari

Iran's supreme leader, Ayatollah Khamenei, does not like criticism and, according to people who know him, he holds lifelong grudges. Of course, holding grudges in old age can exacerbate one's psychological and physical maladies. So, after the rigged presidential election in June 2009, the old tyrant decided to get rid of all the domestic critics of his tyrannical rule. Khamenei thought that by unleashing his supporters in the Islamic Revolutionary Guards Corps and paramilitary Basij he could oppress a great number of people in a very short time. It was a ridiculously impossible task, but despots are not known for their clear understanding of realities.

Khamenei's plan miserably and quickly failed, but that did not stop him from brutalising his people (for some reason, the sound of crushing bones and cracking skulls are music to the ears of dictators). Yet Khamenei and the Guards' intoxication with power did away with any claim to legitimacy the supreme leader had previously enjoyed, and has made him and his regime less sure of their own survival.

Alexis de Tocqueville famously said that the most critical moment for bad governments is the one which witnesses their first steps toward reform. The wrong Tocquevillian lesson would be repeating the same mistakes. Alas, Khameni is doing exactly that. The Iranian regime is making the lives of its citizens as insecure as possible through arbitrary arrests, interrogation, harassment and confiscation of property. Both the regime and the people are reaching boiling point, and the situation is untenable. Even President Ahmadinejad, who was elected with Khamenei's help, has been critical of the regime. During the attack on the British Embassy in November 2011, Ahmadinejad's supporters were quite critical of what happened, while the president himself remained silent. No one regards Ahmadinejad as a sincere opponent of the regime, but he does not want to be on a sinking ship.

An increasing number of Iranians are demanding a transparent and accountable government. The main problem in Iran so far has been that all the governments that have ruled the country have believed that their power has been bestowed by God and that they are accountable only to the Almighty. The former Shah of Iran used to call himself 'the Shadow of God'. Khamenei's supporters regard him as 'Allah's representative on earth'. These titles essentially mean that people's votes and decisions are worthless.

Yet despite their utter disdain for people's votes, autocrats love to be popular. Every few months, Khamenei's people spend millions of dollars bringing together a large number of people from different provinces and asking them to shout slogans such as 'We are ready to die for you, Our Leader' or 'The blood in our veins is dedicated to Our Leader.' Some members of these crowds may genuinely regard their lives as less worthy than Khamenei's, but in my view most of them take part in these gatherings for both the perks and for fear of punishment. I know for a fact that pro-Khamenei demonstrators receive bonuses and extra food rations, and that government employees who refuse to 'dedicate their blood to the leader' can lose their jobs.

Khamenei and some members of his regime have become delusional and it seems that they really do not understand that if they continue to carry out the actions that they have been taking for the past 33 years, the Islamic regime cannot survive for much longer. Imprisoning peaceful critics and imprisoning and torturing opponents didn't help the Soviet Union. It won't help Khamenei's regime either. ❑

©Maziar Bahari
41(1): 80/81
DOI: 10.1177/0306422012439510
www.indexoncensorship.org

Maziar Bahari is a journalist and filmmaker. He was detained in Evin Prison while covering the elections in 2009. He will be talking about his memoir *Then They Came for Me* (Oneworld) with Jon Snow at an *Index*-sponsored event at the Hay Festival on 3 June

FREE SPEECH: THE NEXT 40 YEARS

STRIP SEARCH by MARTIN ROWSON

Summer 2012

(A)S INDEX ON CENSORSHIP celebrates its 40th Birthday, news breaks of Government plans to OUTLAW any expression of GRUMPINESS or ANY EMOTION short of HYSTERICAL ELATION during the DIAMOND JUBILEE & THE OLYMPICS!!

Luckily the plans collapse when a *small child* takes ONE LOOK at Her Majesty! Denied an Anti-Grumpiness Law, the Govt. rushes through law to ban DISCUSSION OF THE ECONOMY instead...

CHEER UP MUM!

EOW FARK AWF THE FLEEMING LAWT OF YEW!

HEY! SOME CLOWN RECKONS WE'LL GET 0.00001% GROWTH IN Q3!

YOU ARE FUCKING NICKED!!

FINANCIAL TIMES
completely fucked

2015 Despite the ECONOMY CHAT BAN, the World Economy TANKS anyway. The only money left is now ALL in the hands of 12 HEDGE FUND managers — who BUY the WORLD's MEDIA to meet their own needs...

Davos Divas
ELITE YACHT
Cocaine News
FILTH RICH
FATCAT FUN
CAPITAL PIG

2017 Increasing unrest leads to many countries bringing in harsh laws ENFORCING UNFOUNDED HAPPINESS...

ACTUALLY, EVERYTHING'S SHIT!

2020 Though ANTI-MISERY LAWS are soon widely flouted by new post-digital TEEN CRAZE known on the streets as "THINKING"...

2025 Emergency Summit of World Leaders to regulate "THINKING" leads directly to eruption of WORLD SPRING....

BIT OF BLUE SKY THINKING HERE, GUYS, BUT HOW ABOUT WE JUST **KILL THE KIDS?**

BRILLIANT! HUZZAH!

WE'RE SAVED!

HAPPY DAYS ARE HERE AGAIN!

HEPPY BEERTH-DIE T'ME! NOW DRAIN ME ANOTHER VIRGIN AND DON'T STINT ON THE GRATED MONKEY GLANDS!

2031 After 6 long years of struggle the GLOBAL INSURRECTION TRIUMPHS! But in *all* the excitement no one notices that a *mysteriously* rejuvenated RUPERT MURDOCH celebrates 100th birthday by *PATENTING SLEEP* and launching exclusive PAY-PER-DREAM SUBSCRIPTION PACKAGE!!

2032 The Global SLEEP STRIKE leads to increased GRUMPINESS & consequent growth in quite uncalled for FOUL LANGUAGE! Religious Groups demand tough new *Anti-Talking-Out-Loud* LAWS!

GOD I'M FUCKING TIRED!

KILL THE BLASPHEMER!!

2052 After 20 long years Humanity finally has a snooze when Murdoch's LIFE FORCE, now an *APP*, is accidentally deleted by a *typically* hopeless CHILD/LACKEY CLONE! Universal rejoicing at final achievement of FULL FREEDOM OF EXPRESSION, just in time for INDEX's 80th BIRTHDAY!!! And, as VENUS is aligned to URANUS over the Clerkenwell LEY LINE, every time a tiny child lisps the word **INDEX** magical UNICORNS appear from nowhere, choired by SINGING PUPPIES!!!

FAAAARK

INDEX is *INSTANTLY BANNED* under HEALTH & SAFETY LAWS!! To be cont?

New books from the Arab World

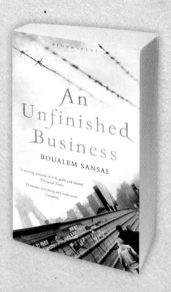

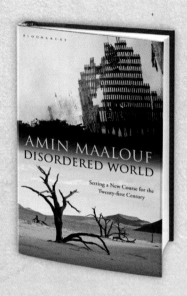

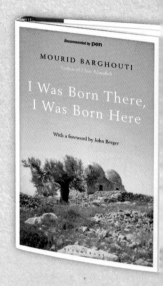

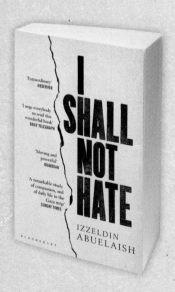

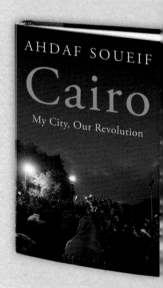

BLOOMSBURY

CODES OF CONDUCT

Irena Maryniak considers the hidden network of relationships that continue to shape Russian society, undermine the rule of law and protect the status quo

About five years before the Soviet Union toppled, as long repressed thoughts and memories began to emerge in the public domain, an underground rock group from the Urals produced a runaway hit crying out against the stifling power of enforced communality. The song, by the band Nautilus Pompilius, has been compared to Pink Floyd's single 'Another Brick in the Wall'. It was called 'Bound by One Chain' and denounced the restrictive, impersonal bonds of collective obligation that had assured the conformism and stability of Soviet society for seven decades: 'I reach for a hand but get an elbow, I search for eyes but feel a gaze ... Bound by one chain, tied by one goal ...'

In fact the Soviet population was fettered not by a single ideological chain but by many. People functioned under the watchful eye of the Communist Party and the state, but they were also linked by intricate bonds of interpersonal relations and informal codes designed to circumvent the system and provide whatever was in short supply. Lives were tightly and inextricably connected and everyone was dependent on their network, the favours they could give and the favours they took. The patronage and support offered might be illegal or legal, but it was hard to stay wholly within the law so the possibility of selective punishment was forever pending. Who knew when a temporarily submerged rule would come up and bite?

In March 1989, when *glasnost* and *perestroika* seemed increasingly well established, I was sent by *Index* to a city regarded by some as the ancient heart of Russia: Kiev, the centre of early medieval Rus' and now the capital of independent Ukraine. It was the third anniversary of the nuclear explosion at Chernobyl, less than 60 miles away, and my assignment was to talk to nationalist and environmental activists about identities and loyalties, and the implications of what had happened. I came away a week later with memories of interrupted interviews in parks or crowded cellar cafes, and of green demonstrations where shadowy figures in leather coats and homburg hats flitted through the crowd questioning protesters, before engaging in friendly chat with heavyweight thugs amusing themselves with serviceable-looking flick knives (*Index* 5/89). But above all, I felt a sense that what had happened to Reactor Number 4 on 26 April 1986 somehow epitomised the lethal fall-out from a system that had failed as much because of flawed communication as – to use a favourite Soviet euphemism – 'for technical reasons'.

It was the communication aspect that fascinated me most. The Soviet experience seemed to produce brilliant raconteurs, ideal interviewees: focused, eager and clear, never at a loss for words, trained from school age to speak out boldly, with a view to making short shrift of the flawed thinking of western capitalists. But now that the apathy and falseness of the system was being exposed, they could step out of the dialectical materialist framework and the moralising that had formed them. People were finally thinking things through and putting them into words, and conversation possessed the intensity and directness of freshly minted ideas seemingly untouched by calculation, agenda or interest.

Gorbachev's reforms were making attempts to overcome the dual pull of party political power and constitutional legality. Political prisoners, serving long terms in labour camps for what they had said or written, were being released. But as a visitor to the Soviet Union, one was still functioning in a system where ideology and connections mattered far more than any written legal code. Under communism, relations between members of the community and their interests were addressed only in so far as they conformed to the expectations of a party-minded 'people's state'. The Communist Party and its associated privileged elite *(nomenklatura)* came first, alongside the security apparatus and the army. Everyone else – that is to say a majority of about 200 million – was expected to follow deferentially. In a failing economy people survived by clinging to an untold mass of informal arrangements and commitments through which they secured milk, fruit, sausage, jeans,

Nautilus Pompilius's lead singer celebrates the 25th anniversary of the hit single 'Bound by One Chain', Moscow, December 2008
Credit: Ria Novosti

Beatles LPs or the latest unofficially published novel. Overhanging this was the shadow of another kind of law associated with the certainties of state-protected privilege, immoveable position and power. Those who possessed these certainties knew they would never walk alone because they formed an integral part of the body of the state, and – unless loyalty was breached – the state guaranteed to protect them.

They seemed nebulous, humourless figures who somehow didn't quite merge with the crowd, but looked well-nourished, confident, and in control. The guy in a good suit towering over everyone else in a Moscow metro carriage; the perfectly turned out young woman assisting at an international conference; the unobtrusive, seemingly approachable hotel porter whose eyes narrowed when he was asked to point to the nearest bus-stop ('Where exactly do you want to go?'); the athletic-looking student at Moscow State University whose softly spoken sister offered tea and jam in perfect porcelain cups, and who remarked, though not to me: 'Ah yes ... the forbidden fruit is sweet.' Or those innocuous seeming figures who emerged unexpectedly from the crowd and tapped your arm as you picked at a bowl of watery stewed fruit in the Lenin Library canteen: 'I remember you. You were at Yurii Kariakin's lecture.' (Flattering, because the event had been attended by hundreds; yet this couldn't be a chat-up line – he was already gone.) Or else as you disembarked from the metro at Revolution Square: 'I recognise that coat. It's Polish.' (Not so – though my name is ... but she had vanished into the crowd.)

In Kiev, Oles Shevchenko, a political prisoner of eight years standing, reassured me: 'On the whole the KGB don't touch people these days. But we do tend to be followed. Don't worry. Ignore them.' I did, but how could you ever know who was who? 'I search for eyes but feel a gaze,' Nautilus Pompilius intoned ... Everyone was watching, looking-out for ... what? And if they weren't, they were doing a pretty good job pretending. Conversation was periodically interspersed with an absent, tuneful little hum – 'uhuu' – which might mean anything but seemed to say: 'That's your story. But I know. I've seen. You can't fool me. I'm watching.'

How did one function in all this? There was the preparation: no international calls – they were said to be uniformly bugged; names of contacts were acquired through Russian networks in the West or from earlier visitors. And while everyone talked of openness and restructuring, there were slightly chill warnings from Soviet émigrés, whose experience made their remarks hard to ignore: 'They follow you in threes. At customs, look confident, make sure your knees aren't knocking. They have mirrors. They check.'

Once through the customs hurdle, it was a question of memorising maps and directions; using public telephones, never calling from hotel rooms; arranging to meet at a metro station ('I'll be by the first carriage, carrying a copy of *Ogonyok*') or under a monument ('I'll be wearing a dark hat and sunglasses' – was he having me on?). I'd choose unlikely routes; slip off

1986 – South Africa

Journalists are prohibited from reporting at the scene of 'any unrest, restricted gathering or security action' under emergency regulations introduced in June. The crackdown coincides with the 10th anniversary of the student uprising against apartheid in Soweto.

the trolleybus last; walk down unlit pathways and deserted patches of forest in between apartment blocks in search of an address brought into the country in a sock or tucked away under a bra strap. There'd be that pointless precautionary look back, before diving into an apartment block entrance, and I'd arrive, often unannounced, bearing gifts: the latest Margaret Atwood, coffee, tights, soap, eau de cologne, a new John Updike. I walked into people's lives like some kind of untested catalytic agent offering promises of a readership, exposure, links with a free world, in exchange for thoughts and beliefs that were offered on trust. And I'd leave with tapes, notes and typed sheets which I'd spread around my bags or about my person before venturing back to the airport.

The crumbling Soviet system brought jubilation, discomfiture and intense uncertainty. 'In this country social disturbance means a bloodbath,' the widely-respected official literary critic Lev Anninsky told me in 1987. 'That's why we have always kept our society so tightly reined, and that's why there is so much anxiety now that the reins appear to be looser.'

Even dissenters like Leonid Borodin, just released from five years' imprisonment when I visited him in his Moscow flat, complained of the confusion that *glasnost* brought. 'In open opposition things seemed clearer,' he said. 'It was easier to understand where we stood. Now there's nothing with which to oppose *perestroika* and in a way we have been proved wrong.'

As former editor Sally Laird observed in *Index* at the time, the boundaries between 'official' and 'unofficial' had 'begun subtly to shift'. Ideological slogans and the upright thinking designed to resist the 'ideological-cultural aggression of imperialism' were colliding with expressions of interior experience and an overwhelming sense of the absurd. People read about the Stalinist labour camps in official magazines; listened to the BBC, Voice of America and Radio Liberty, danced to songs denouncing state hypocrisy and conformism; told jokes about the system, and walked to the metro past billboards pasted with scarlet slogans: 'Lenin lived, lives and evermore shall live.'

Soviet citizens were in constant contact with 'the powerful magnetic field of ideological influence', the émigré Alexander Zinoviev wrote. 'They absorb from it a certain electric charge ... There is physically no way they can escape from it.' In practice, though, ideology was less about political and economic ideas than about collectivity and loyalty: to the Party, the state and the leadership that embodied it. In a sense, Vladimir Putin, who publicly lamented the fall of the Soviet Union as 'one of the greatest geopolitical catastrophes of the 20th century', has continued to carry this 'electric charge' for over a decade now, with ideological and free market ways of addressing issues running in tandem. Though the economic principles of

In memory of Sally Laird: 1956-2010

Sally Laird became editor of *Index on Censorship* in August 1988, following the death of George Theiner. A scholar of Russian, educated at Oxford and Harvard, she had already spent two years as the magazine's specialist on Soviet affairs, covering the rise of *perestroika*. Her tenure as editor was brief (one year only) but it coincided with a momentous period of history: the Rushdie affair, Tiananmen Square and the Velvet Revolution were some of the memorable highlights. Evidently, there was much to talk about. Sally inherited an ethos that suited her; then, as now, the magazine was notable for the width and sobriety of its coverage. Though the issues involved were naturally emotive – as emotive as can be, in many cases – one could rely on *Index* to gather the facts objectively and to set them out in painstaking detail. This didn't mean that opinion was absent – rather, that it was latent, and belonged (invisibly, as it were) to the magazine's liberal remit. Sally was an excellent writer – an essay on 'Writers under Gorbachev' was widely cited; and she encouraged journalism that was personal, sceptical and spiced with elegant humour. These, at any event, were her own qualities, beautifully brought to the fore in an essay like 'Prague Autumn' (January 1989), where she recounted a visit to the Czech capital in the company of a group of Charter 77 activists, in order to seek out and make contact with Václav Havel. In this wry, funny, self-deprecating piece, she described photographing Havel's arrest by the secret police, only to suffer the indignity of having the film promptly ripped out of her camera. At the end of the year – a year in so many ways of extraordinary hope and excitement – she left *Index* to help set up a new Central and East European publishing project funded by George Soros, before moving to Denmark in the early 90s to work there as a full-time translator and writer. I remember those far-off times vividly: 1989 was the year of my courtship. I met Sally in the month she was appointed editor. And in the month she quit the magazine, I married her.

Mark Le Fanu

Marxism have been shaken off, the principle of group dependence, high expectations of mutual help from friends, exchange of favours, shared responsibility, and conformity still prevail alongside the time-honoured ethos of pervasive rule violation and selective punishment. Despite a more synchronised and potentially effective system of legislation introduced under Putin, individual interests remain subordinate to collective ones. People are driven by the rules and the *mores* of the group that nurtures them. Russians call it '*krugovaia poruka*', a protective mutual guarantee. Political, professional and business practices remain based on interpersonal trust, mutual surveillance and a code of discipline more likely to be enforced by an informal network than by the law. And, at a political level, an ideology of absolute loyalty to the Kremlin has been enshrined within the code of conduct expected of state agencies and public figures. Any threat to the status quo and to the functioning of these agencies is ruthlessly addressed.

The journalist Anna Politkovskaya, murdered in the lift of her Moscow apartment block in October 2006, was particularly suspicious of the effects of the Kremlin's reach, especially the leadership's dialogue with opponents: 'It is a recurrent Russian problem: proximity to the Kremlin makes people slow to say no, and altogether less discriminating,' she wrote in *A Russian Diary*. 'The Kremlin knows this full well ... First they are gently clasped to the authorities' breast. In Russia the best way to subjugate even the most recalcitrant is not money, but bringing us in from the cold ... The rebellious soon begin to subside.'

Politkovskaya did a great deal to expose the more murky workings of post-Soviet Russia, particularly the abuses and censorship associated with the Second Chechen War, initiated in 1999. Her frontline reports for *Novaya Gazeta* covered summary executions, kidnapping, disappearances, rape and torture, inflicted on the Chechen population by the Russian armed forces and the Russian-backed administration of Akhmad Kadyrov. Measures had already been taken at the time to ensure that the media could not embarrass the authorities with reports questioning their methods and credibility. The lawyer now representing Politkovskaya's family, Karina Moskalenko, is currently dealing with a host of still unresolved cases relating to human rights abuses in Chechnya and attacks by the federal armed forces on local populations. 'These actions have never been investigated,' she tells me. 'Cases relating to these issues get to court only very rarely, and journalists who help people to obtain legal aid, human rights activists, lawyers and activists who assist victims seeking legal reparations are being killed in Russia.' She mentions Stanislav

Markelov, a human rights lawyer who fought against discrimination and judicial malpractice while representing Anna Politkovskaya, and was shot by a masked gunman after giving a press conference in January 2009. A trainee journalist, Anastasya Baburova, was also killed in the attack. She recalls the mysterious death of investigative journalist Yuri Shchekochikhin. As his family's designated lawyer, she is fighting to have the case investigated as a murder. (There has been speculation about possible radioactive poisoning.)

'In Russia, impunity begins and ends with the unaccountability of the state,' Moskalenko says. 'The investigation into Politkovskaya's murder collapsed on absolutely unacceptable, unprofessional grounds. Answers to crucial questions have not been given and responsibilities neglected. Some people – who may have been present when the killing took place, or not – came to be incorrectly accused. They wanted to lay the blame for everything on them – something which we, as representatives of Anna Politkovskaya's family, simply could not allow. We demanded a real investigation … Yuri Shchekochikhin did not die of an unknown illness but was murdered because he was a journalist, a human rights activist, as well as a member of parliament and co-chairman of the Committee for the Battle against Corruption. He was deprived of his life because he fought against these kinds of abuses. And since that there has been no effective or timely investigation into his case, it is more and more difficult to establish the truth.'

When Alexander Litvinenko was murdered in London in November 2006, Russian state television reported the story with references to Politkovskaya's killing a month earlier and the shooting, in 2004, of Paul Khlebnikov, editor of the Russian edition of *Forbes* magazine. It was implied that all three deaths were associated with underground networks of illegal business and ex-KGB operatives – though this also diverted attention from any suggestion that these (and other unexplained or violent deaths of journalists, human rights activists and lawyers) might be in any way connected with the Kremlin.

1989 – Iran

Ayatollah Khomeini issues a fatwa against Salman Rushdie, sentencing him and all those involved in the publication of his novel *The Satanic Verses* to death. In 1998, President Khatami's government announces that it does not support the death threat against Rushdie.

Of course the presence of disgruntled ex-KGB operatives in the community, after the dissolution of the Soviet Union in 1991, did create a climate in which informal leverage was constantly being exercised to discredit or destroy competitors, enemies and opponents. Boris Yeltsin's fragmentation of the Soviet security system left tens of thousands of former security officers jobless. It is estimated that in the early 1990s more than 50,000 ex-KGB agents joined private security firms taking with them considerable know-how, a not insignificant proportion of their former employer's technology of surveillance, and long-standing connections. With a push to the market accompanied by very little management, and inconsistent or contradictory legislation, the pressure to respect informal codes in preference to formal juridical rules was overwhelming. 'Everybody who did not spend the last decade staying in bed has willingly or unwillingly violated the law', Boris Berezovsky reportedly remarked in 2000. Not everyone, however, had to take the legal consequences. At a high political level the existing legal system could be manipulated to its limits by savvy political consultants. Telephone law – informal requests phoned through from the Kremlin – tended to be far more efficiently enforced than formal rules.

'The rigidity of our laws is compensated for by their non-observance,' Russians like to say. Yet continuing juridical malpractice, and the fact that legal decisions are often taken hand in glove with the state authorities, mean that in cases when fundamental legal issues are at stake neither the plaintiff nor the defendant can rely on a fair trial. Karina Moskalenko calls it 'a catastrophic state of affairs'. But, most recently, the desire for legal recourse has led many to look outside Russia. Moskalenko is director of the International Protection Centre (IPC), which provides legal aid to victims of human rights violations applying to the European Court of Human Rights (ECHR), in Strasbourg, or the UN Human Rights Committee, in Geneva. The IPC receives between 300 and 1000 appeals against the Russian state authorities every month, of which hundreds are passed onto the ECHR. More than 160 cases have been won. Moskalenko believes that the effect on public consciousness is palpable.

'Stereotypes are being destroyed. People are beginning to understand that they need not rely wholly on the authorities. They can take care of their own defence. Equally the authorities in some cases acknowledge the justice of the rulings and change the system, though at times they simply pay out compensation and continue the same practice. That is why, today, the Council of Europe is having to address the issue of the non-implementation of ECHR decisions ... But it seems to me that Russians are waking up. The ECHR cannot replace the Russian legal system, it can only decide on cases.

Anna Politkovskaya's son Ilya and lawyer Karina Moskalenko at a district military court after the jury acquits four people for the journalist's murder, 19 February 2009.
Credit: Ria Novosti

It can only rule where human rights have been infringed and where they haven't. But the very fact that such a judicial agency exists, and the availability of this procedure, holds the authorities back. People cease to be as helpless as they were, or so wholly in the hands of state agencies ...'

In addition, as the legal academic Alexei Trochev has pointed out, Russia's membership of the Council of Europe has helped support the independence of the Russian courts from law enforcement authorities and strengthened their judicial power in the sense of requiring government agencies to carry out court decisions. The increase in the use of courts by Russians has been dramatic. Even though in 2001 just 23 per cent of the population said they trusted the courts, the last decade has seen a doubling of civil cases in Russia. When powerful business or political interests are involved, however, the legal system remains at the disposal of the authorities. The Kremlin dictates and telephone law prevails. The widely reported case of the oil giant Yukos is emblematic. Unwritten rules had been violated: the head of the company, Mikhail Khodorkovsky (arrested in 2003 on charges of tax evasion, fraud and embezzlement) had not stayed out of politics. He had financed opposition parties; he had bought too much influence in the State Duma and declared participation in the 2008 elections. He broke the rules of *krugovaia poruka* and is currently serving a prison sentence extended to 14 years.

Long established and routine informal practices undermine the rule of law in Russia. They also impede free speech, media independence and the principle of fair elections. But as Alena Ledeneva has pointed out in her book *How Russia Really Works*, unofficial support networks also entrap the regime itself. The authorities are as dependent on the controls of *krugovaia poruka* as ordinary Russian citizens, who have demonstrated since last December against vote rigging and electoral fraud in the parliamentary and presidential elections. Obstacles to the establishment of the rule of law, unprescribed public discourse, and democratic development are being incessantly reproduced, at every level, by a traditional and intrinsically noxious subsystem of cultivated protectionism and partiality. ❏

©Irena Maryniak
41(1): 85/95
DOI: 10.1177/0306422012439155
www.indexoncensorship.org

Irena Maryniak is former Eastern Europe editor of *Index on Censorship* and a regular contributor

CZECHOSLOVAK 'BLACK LIST'

NAMES OF AUTHORS THAT SHOULD NOT BE MENTIONED IN CONNECTION WITH THE 50TH ANNIVERSARY OF THE FOUNDATION OF THE COMMUNIST PARTY.

Those who have emigrated:

Josef Škvorecký	Vrat. Blažek	A.J. Liehm
Arnošt Lustig	Lad. Mňačko	Ota Šik
Lad. Grossmann	Ludvik Aškenázy	Luděk Šnepp
Ivan Diviš	Milan Schulz	Ed. Goldstücker
Ant. Brousek		

Those who have organized opposition against the party:

Jan Procházka	Pavel Kohout	Ivan Klíma
Jan Drda	Lud Vaculík	Milan Kundera
Václav Havel		

Those who have taken up anti-party positions and have been struck out or expelled from the party and have not yet changed their point of view:

Jan Otčenášek	Josef Láník	Jan Stuchl
Jiří Šotola	Vlad. Pzourek	Stanislav Vejvoda
Karel Šiktanc	Lad. Ptáčnik	Vlad. Vávra
Lad. Bublík	Jiří Žák	Gustav Bare
Alena Bernáškova	Mojmír Klánský	Adolf Branald
Mirosl. Červenka	Ivan Kříž	Jan Drda
Arnošt Lustig	Jiří Kupka	Eduard Hončík
Jan Šigut	Václav Lacina	Jarmila Otradovicová
Oldřich Suléř	Jan Martinec	Jos. Pros
Anna Třesohlavová	Fr. Neužil	Karel Ptáčník
Arnošt Vaněček	Fr. Rachlík	Lenka Hašková
Lucien Wichs	Lenka Reinerová	Jan Kopecký
Hana Bělohradská	Vlad. Remeš	Ivan Kubíček
Oldřich Daněk	Anna Sedlmayerová	Milan Kyselý
Mojmír Grygar	Fr. Směja	

Poets:

Ilja Bart	Ivo Fleischmann	Karel Šiktanc
Miroslav Červenka	Boris Jachnin	Jiří Šotola
Lumír Čivrný	Zdeněk Kriebel	Jan Štern
Miroslav Fikrle	Jaroslav Seifert	

SLOVAK AUTHORS:

Those who have emigrated or have been expelled:	Those who have been criticized:
L. Mňačko	L. Tážký
E. Štefan	D. Tatarka
R. Kukálek	A. Hykiš
T. Fiš	M. Ferko
D. Monoszly	P. Karvaš — *(resigned his function in the Writer's Union)*

THELONGVIEW

Czech writer **Ludvík Vaculík** on a formative
encounter with censorship in his youth

In April 1988 I wrote an article for *Index on Censorship* describing my lengthy
and all-encompassing experience of censorship under the old regime. I ended
it with the view that censorship taught us in that era to write inventively
and our readers to read shrewdly. Then, though, I mentioned censorship as
concerning people writing or talking to the general public. But limiting freedom can also affect other forms of expression: painting, filmmaking and even
music. We saw that with our own eyes. It even affected fashion and hairstyles.

I actually encountered censorship for the first time as a youth at a Bata
Shoe Company residential block when I wrote something meant to amuse
my friends at a meeting of the collective. I think it was in 1943, the fifth year
of the war. Food, clothing and shoes were all rationed. As a result, there
were few pairs of shoes to be had, which was felt even by us who helped
to manufacture them. At the time I was allocated to leather working boots
with rubber soles: I hammered little iron horseshoes into the soles. It was
decent work.

In the summer of that year we received an order at the young workers´
hall of residence that we had to wear wooden sandals. They were cheap
clogs with straps. Not really bad to walk in. As a rule, instructors stood at the
residence's exit and checked us over: we had to wear a tie or an open-necked
shirt, clean boots, a hat (in winter) and a company emblem (B in a circle). We
also had to have those wooden clogs. They clattered on the cobblestoned
pavements and sometimes they were slippy. I am not sure where I came up
with the song:

> When the first cobbler was born, a jolly wheeze it was,
> Everyone rushed to see the wee shoe-making boss.
> A shoe-making wizard without a doubt
> Making sure we don´t find some barefooted lout.

I then added the following:

> We Bata-folk make countless sounds shoes to flog,
> But surprise surprise we toddle off just in a clog.
> If this carries on we won't be clattering much longer,
> We'll take the bull by the horns, don't think we'll linger.
> And sing:
> Barefoot across Labour Square you'll hear our soft taps.
> After all, we're no Bata pioneering saps.

The song was in the tune of a Czech traditional folk song. My success was assured! The instructor, though, took me aside and told me I was witty but it wasn't the right thing to do. I should mull over as to why the order was given. Responsible people are trying to find a solution to the problem of shortages. Clogs are not a shortcoming fashion that deserves to be mocked. Besides which, to take the mickey out of one's own company? And I shouldn't take it as censorship. I think that it was that moment that this started to gnaw at me: I'd discovered self-censorship...

Today, when we have an almost unhindered freedom of expression, we see much more in the way of complaints of censorship than when it wasn't allowed. I receive readers' letters at the magazine I edit with complaints that a certain newspaper has refused to publish their article. They are always run-of-the-mill and banal pieces of general abuse (sometimes valid) lacking the realisation that the subject is in fact being written about all over the place.

Today's adorable free speech attracts attention and seduces susceptible people to never-ending babble... I think that too little attention is given to another freedom: the freedom to act. ❏

Translated by Pavel Theiner
©Ludvík Vaculík
41(1): 96/98
DOI: 10.1177/0306422012438664
www.indexoncensorship.org

Ludvík Vaculík is a leading Czech writer and was a regular contributor to *Index* in the communist era. He was the author of a famous manifesto for reform in 1968 and a signatory of Charter 77

CYBER HOLES

Andrej Dynko

The world watched the public displays of weeping for Kim Jong-il from a safe distance. Were the North Koreans really crying or were they performing at gunpoint? 'After all, they've got the internet and satellite TV, haven't they?' wrote one young innocent in the comments on the YouTube clip.

Yes, kids, many of our age group in such countries really do weep and wail and wonder how they are ever going to live without their Beloved Leader.

To those of us who have the resources and the ability to compare, Kim seems a grotesque, brutal dwarf and his son a fat, presumptuous slob. Fat means vile in a country where, from hunger and hopelessness, so many people are as thin as ghosts.

To us, but not to North Koreans, who are not able to compare.

Indeed, if a North Korean is ordered to launch nuclear missiles at 'the imperialists and their puppets', which could even lead to the destruction of mankind, they will be proud to obey the orders of their Beloved Leader.

'That is possible in North Korea because of their mentality, which has been fostered by Confucianism,' is one explanation you hear.

'It all results from the psychological trauma of the Korean War,' left-wingers tell us.

Fortunately, that is untrue. There is no such thing as a national predisposition to dictatorship. It is neither an Asian nor an eastern phenomenon. The most brutal dictatorships have arisen in Europe. No one is safe from tyranny. The 'captive mind', as Nobel Prize-winner Czeslaw Milosz called it, is universal.

There was the same grief, the same crowds in Moscow, in 1953 when Stalin died, only 59 years ago. If Hitler had died of a heart attack, would not just as many tears have been shed in Berlin? And my own Belarus, our quiet, cosy little dictatorship, is a reminder that it is all still possible in Europe, once an individual maniacally obsessed with power gets into government.

What really struck me about the sparse footage from Pyongyang was the obsessive cleanliness of the streets. It strongly reminds me of the orderliness in Minsk, in which the Belarusian regime takes such pride and which is so admired by visitors from countries with a chaotic political life. I mention this because dictatorship can be deceptively attractive.

Even testimony about atrocities committed by the Kims, like those of Gaddafi or Lukashenko, is often exaggerated. The unwelcome truth is that with electronic media, and electronic mind benders, relatively small doses of violence are enough to keep people in check. It is easier than ever to reduce people to slaves. The North Koreans and Chinese are living testimony.

Sometimes even dire need is not enough to sow doubt in captive minds, such is the condition of intellectual isolation. Freedom is not just having the opportunity to compare, but also having the ability to compare.

The examples of West and East Germany, North and South Korea show that the society which lives in freedom attains technological and economic superiority, with the result that dictatorships are doomed to fail. The success of West Germany and of South Korea would have been impossible, however, without the aid of the United States. Accordingly, the Free World must continue to systematically support its outposts against the dictators and sow the seeds of freedom in the 'realm of darkness'. As for Belarus, its future depends on how Poland and Ukraine develop.

It is idle to hope that efforts will produce instant results everywhere. The Lukashenko regime, for example, is capable of standing still for a long time yet, thanks to its sponsors in Moscow.

The government of any country can, if it wishes, easily block access to the internet, including social networks – just as easily as the Soviet regime jammed Radio Liberty and the BBC. But through the infernal noise people made out voices and were able to hear something. In developed countries radio has been superseded by the internet, so today the free world should methodically develop tools to make it easier to drill holes through cyberwalls. At the same time, it should work systematically on ways of delivering information to closed societies, even if that requires superhuman efforts. ❏

Translated by Arch Tait
©Andrej Dynko
41(1): 100/101
DOI: 10.1177/0306422012438312
www.indexoncensorship.org

Andrej Dynko is editor of *Nasha Niva*, one of the few remaining independent newspapers in Belarus

POETS

Children's Writers

Scientists

HISTORIANS

Novelists

Daydreamers

Comedians

MUSICIANS

imagine the world

The Telegraph
HAY FESTIVAL

sky ARTS HD
BROADCAST SPONSOR

31 MAY TO 10 JUNE 2012

HAYFESTIVAL.ORG

AFRICA AMERICAS ASIA EUROPE MIDDLE EAST

Zapis editors detained

Among the numerous intellectuals detained or arrested by the military regime of General Jaruzelski following the imposition of martial law in Poland in early December are several editors and contributors of the unofficial literary quarterly *Zapis*.

The first editor of the journal, one of Poland's most respected writers and poets, Wiktor Woroszylski was arrested at the Ursus tractor factory on the outskirts of Warsaw when this was raided by the security forces who broke up the workers' strike. Together with KOR member Jan Józef Lipski (a well-known contributor to *Zapis*) Woroszylski went to Ursus to show solidarity with the workers and to take part in a debate. Both were dragged out by security men and have been charged under the martial law regulations which carry penalties of up to 15 years imprisonment. While Wiktor Woroszylski is in Mokotow Prison in Warsaw, Jan Józef Lipski has suffered a heart attack and is in hospital under military guard.

Jacek Bocheński, the current editor of *Zapis*, was detained for about a week but then released after he refused to sign the 'loyalty pledge' demanded by the authorities. Bocheński crossed out the words by which the signatory undertakes 'not to act against the interests of the Polish Republic' (as this can be seen as a tacit admission of having done so in the past) and instead wrote 'I have never acted against the interests of the Polish Republic, and never shall'.

Other leading contributors to *Zapis* who are known to be in detention include the poet Anka Kowalska, the actress Halina Mikolajska, the writer Szczypiorski, as well as two of Poland's most famous 'dissidents', Jacek Kuroń and Adam Michnik.

Contrary to some earlier reports of torture and ill-treatment, it seems that Miss Kowalska and Miss Mikolajska, as well as other Polish writers and academics at present in detention, who also include the Secretary General of Polish PEN, Professor Wladyslaw Bartoszewski, are being well treated by the authorities, who appear to reserve rougher treatment for some of the workers and Solidarity members. It is suspected that reports of the torture of Jacek Kuroń and Adam Michnik, for instance, were deliberately spread by the authorities in order to discredit independent, unofficial sources of information. This disinformation comes at a time when the military rulers continue their complete news blackout so that all reports from foreign correspondents in Warsaw have to be submitted for censorship; meanwhile telephone links have not yet been restored.

(*Zapis* first started coming out in Poland in 1977. Produced on duplicating machines in very difficult conditions by the NOWA unofficial publishing house it has 18 issues to date, 16 of which have now been published in London by *Index on Censorship*, which regularly puts out four a year. Wiktor Woroszylski's 'Origins of a Poem' and Andrzej Szczypiorski's 'Poland — the Fiction and the Reality' came out in English in *Index* itself — the special Polish issue, November/December 1979; Anka Kowalska's poem, 'Reason of State', appeared in our 10th anniversary issue in December 1981. *Index* has also prepared a representative list (in English) of the titles put out by NOWA, which is available free on request.)

Index on Censorship

Europe, but its sensitive spot, in which had appeared all the symptoms of diseases long dormant in its organism — which had been violated by arbitrary agreements. Of this character of the Polish crisis both the powers which had concluded those agreements, and were still guaranteeing them, must be made aware; and Poles themselves must know that by suffering economic hunger and carrying an immense risk today, they were acting on behalf of a new European order, though they themselves did not intend to change it. They were working for a new pattern of inter-

are paying the cost of many years' degradation of work and money, and of over-exploitation of all spiritual and material resources. Literature, by descending into the deepest layers of the crisis . . . ought to reveal the devastation, name the moral poverty, and revive in society a movement for rehabilitation and responsibility, not unlike the great reform movements of the past.' Literature, he concluded, ought to 'criticise not only the way Poles are governed, but also the way they live and think'.

Though Andrzej Kijowski is a member of

THELONGVIEW

Philip Spender on the legacy of George Theiner, champion of Czech dissidents

In Prague there is a unique public library called Libri Prohibiti, which contains around 29,000 items by banned Czech and Slovak writers, the majority *samizdat* publications produced in the country under communism. Also on the shelves is a complete set of *Index on Censorship*, because a rich seam of unofficial intellectual life in Czechoslovakia runs through its pages.

This was down to George Theiner, who spent 16 years with the magazine. Steeped in the contemporary culture of his native country, at home with English culture, in daily contact with émigré networks all over the world, communicating with writers inside Czechoslovakia, George presented to the world, via *Index*, the voices of the independent intelligentsia.

He did it by publishing their own words – poems, essays, plays, feuilletons, letters of protest, reportage, short stories, jokes, answers to questionnaires and so on. Almost every piece was prefaced by a short introduction by George. Birthdays and deaths were marked, prizes noted, banned books and writers were listed, censors' reports reprinted, and arrests, trials and jailings tracked.

Virtually all intellectual life was represented – Czechs and Slovaks, young and old, actors, filmmakers, musicians, journalists, academics, publishers and spokesmen for Charter 77, VONS (support group for dissidents) and others; and, in 1978–9, three issues of the unofficial journal *Spektrum* were published by *Index*. These were the people who kept the real Czechoslovak culture alive during the 21 years of repression which followed the Prague Spring. As Václav Havel said after George's death, 'I owe him much gratitude, as do many Czechoslovak writers.'

George joined *Index* as assistant editor to Michael Scammell in 1973. Born in Czechoslovakia, he lived there until just before the war when his father brought the family – Jewish, but not practising Jews – to Britain. Being Czech patriots, the family returned to Prague in 1945 where George, not yet 20, became English language editor of ČTK, the Czechoslovak News Agency,

Index reports on arrest of Polish samizdat journalists (previous page)

George Theiner (right) and Philip Spender in Index's former office in North London

fulfilling his dream of becoming a journalist. The dream ended shortly after the Communist coup of 1948 when George's refusal to join the Party precipitated three years in labour camps and coalmines. In the 50s and 60s he worked as a translator; he also prepared *New Writing in Czechoslovakia* for Penguin, introducing 26 writers.

The fervent hopes of Czechoslovak patriots during the Prague Spring that after 20 years of rigid communism a freer way of life would emerge were obliterated by the Warsaw Pact invasion of August 1968. George discovered his flat was bugged and ripped out the wires. He had had enough and he had an alternative home – Britain. There, during the war, he had spent six and a half years imbibing an English education and falling in love – his words – with its language and literature. English had become his literary language, he had publishing contacts there, and so he drove his family to London.

George was more than a virtuoso with words. He had shared the experiences of those *Index* had been founded to help. He was optimistic, open, witty, humorous and confident about the rightness of the cause. This combination of characteristics, together with a tenacious commitment to the cause of artistic freedom, partly explains why George added so much to the confidence and effectiveness of *Index*'s staff; why his network of friends was so extensive and international; why he got on so well with so many writers both famous and unknown wherever they came from; why so many people made their way to the magazine's office, why its overseas supporters became an active force, why theatre producers and actors in London staged work from the magazine. All of this was meat and drink to George, and it spread wide the work of censored writers and information about their situation.

In 1988, weak from cancer, he accepted in person the Freedom Prize awarded by the newspapers *Dagens Nyheter* of Stockholm and *Politiken* of Copenhagen, delivering a public speech of thanks in Stockholm in fluent Swedish. The same year he was invited to a conference of newspaper editors in South Africa at a time when the press there was under acute pressure from the apartheid government. He said on return it had been one of the most exhilarating experiences of his life. ❏

©Philip Spender
41(1): 104/106
DOI: 10.1177/0306422012438654
www.indexoncensorship.org

Philip Spender worked at *Index* from 1972–1996, starting out in distribution. He was later director and publisher of the magazine

THOUGHTS ON FASTING

Chen Wei's essay was used as evidence against him when he was imprisoned in China last December for nine years for 'inciting subversion of state power'

Today, 10 December 2010, is Human Rights Day, a day bound to be remembered by many – some with joy, some with dismay. Human Rights Day this year is particularly significant for me and I am moved to write to express the emotions welling up inside me. Freud would have called it catharsis. Sima Qian, the Han dynasty historian, reminds us that the writings of ancient China's sages were often prompted by anger. I am no sage, but in these dark circumstances what can I resort to but words?

While at university I participated in the 1989 democracy movement. Most of the students in that movement were, like me, full of idealism and hopes for something better – we had no far-reaching goals of opposing the Party or society as a whole. From elementary school onwards we had been brainwashed to believe the Party represented the people, that it was a progressive force. Add in the economic growth of the mid and late 1980s brought about by reform and opening-up, and we were by nature supporters of the government of the time. But we were too trusting of the propaganda. We actually believed we were the masters of the nation, the hope of the future – and so presumed to give the authorities a few suggestions: punish the corruption that was starting to appear, make society a little more free, open up that tightly closed window just a crack. But clearly both the intellectuals and we students were too naive – how could a regime that regarded the realm as its own private property tolerate such a challenge? So the massacre of 4 June became inevitable. Today we see clearly the nature of the regime – but in 1989 many, particularly the students, did not. They believed the government was sure to understand their well meant aspirations.

I was on Beijing's street in the early morning of 4 June. Nobody could have seen everything that happened, but the tanks and armoured cars charging past, the assault rifles spitting fire, and the students fallen at my side were enough to awaken me from that dream. My understanding of China was shattered. I realised what the authorities strive to hide: we are not the masters of our nation, a one-party dictatorship is, and democracy is no more than a fig leaf. Neither wishing nor daring to implement democracy, they talk of national circumstances and East-West differences. So what if it's in the constitution? The right to interpret that constitution lies with those who stand against democracy.

Fasting became one weapon to use in my struggle. For many years I was imprisoned, unable to write and tell the world what I thought of this dark system or to mourn the fallen of 4 June. But on that day every year I fasted – that was one right I could not have taken from me.

Twenty years have passed. There has been hardship and confusion, but I have neither regretted nor shrunk from my path. Not because I have courage or lofty ideals – I just want to show that an ordinary man can sustain his contempt for a powerful autocracy; I just want to use a lifetime of persistence to redeem my now weakened conscience. My lack of fear is not because there is no threat – it is because the fear I feel is nothing compared to the call of my conscience. When arrested after 4 June I told myself I would face up to right and wrong – even if I could not speak the whole truth, I would not utter one lie nor ignore my conscience. No matter if I am in jail, no matter

1989 – China

On 3-4 June, the communist government puts an abrupt end to weeks of pro-democracy demonstrations in Beijing's Tiananmen Square, opening fire and killing hundreds of people. There are mass arrests, with student leaders targeted. The massacre leads to international sanctions.

认定上述事实的证据如下：

物证、书证，证人证言，被告人供述，

检查记录，电子证物检查工作记录等。

本院认为，被告人陈卫以在互联网公开发表文章

方式煽动颠覆国家政权，推翻社会主义制度，其行为

华人民共和国刑法》第一百零五条第二款之规定，

楚，证据确实充分，应当以煽动颠覆国家政权罪追究

任。被告人陈卫曾因危害国家安全犯罪被判处有期徒

罚执行完毕后，再犯危害国家安全犯罪，依照《中华人

刑法》第六十六条之规定，系累犯，应当从重处罚。依据

人民共和国刑事诉讼法》第一百四十一条的规定，提起公

依法判处。

此致

四川省遂宁市中级人民法院

检察员：李虹志

代理检察员：李 琴

二〇一一年十一月二十五日

被告人陈卫现羁押于遂宁市看守所；

证据目录和证人名单各一份；

how difficult life becomes, no matter if I have to make excuses for an embarrassing lack of money – none of this matters to me. I do not have the power to save everyone in China, but I have saved myself. So I am calm. I stand on unassailable ground.

So much is happening this Human Rights Day I must take things one by one. Liu Xianbin's detention (human rights activist, sentenced to ten years in 2011 for 'inciting subversion of state power') is one of the Chinese government's gravest breaches of human rights in recent years. On 28 July he was taken and later his home was searched. The police took his hard drive, but he was only charged in connection with several openly published articles. We can imagine how disappointed the police were – they must have been sure Liu had been stirring up human rights incidents and public protests from behind the scenes. Proving the connection would discredit the whole human-rights movement: 'Look, you've been had.' But they found no evidence, and had nothing to use against him but those articles.

But Liu Xianbin's arrest ended up with the authorities on the back foot, caught unawares by an unexpected level of protest. 'I am Liu Xianbin' groups sprang up in more than 20 provinces, and support came from both China and overseas. 'Relay Hunger Strikes' took place in China, in Hong Kong and abroad. This reaction to the detention of a Chinese political prisoner was unprecedented, and we can see this as an uprising of the spirit.

By coincidence I am fasting today at the same time as those fasting for Liu Xianbin – or perhaps fate had a hand in it?

Today can also be considered the second anniversary of the 08 Charter. Although it was actually published on 9 December 2008, its drafters originally planned to release it on 10 December – Human Rights Day. But on the 8th, Liu Xiaobo was arrested, and so the charter was published early to avoid any more unforeseen circumstances. So we can regard the 10th as the anniversary of its publication. Over ten thousand Chinese citizens have signed the era-defining 08 Charter over the last two years, demonstrating the hopes

▶▶

1994 – Rwanda

An estimated 800,000 of the country's minority Tutsis and moderate majority Hutus are brutally murdered. Hate speech broadcast on Radio Télévision Libre des Mille Collines and other media is believed to play a significant role in inciting the violence.

of the Chinese people for constitutional democracy. Liu Xianbin signed the charter less than a month after his release, in breach of the conditions of that release – and was delighted to do so. I was also one of the first signatories. To see the democracy movement develop from an isolated challenge to the regime by a few of the brave to a social movement makes me proud. Society is moving forward.

Of course the real focus today is the award ceremony for the Nobel Peace Prize. I was on Liu Xia's (Liu Xiaobo's wife) guest list for the ceremony – a great honour. As much as I wish to be in Oslo to witness the historic moment, the weakened authorities will not allow it. Nobody on the guest list resident in China will be able to attend – a new historic first for our autocrats.

Liu Xiaobo's award sent the authorities into confusion, with no response beyond the same old mouldy rhetoric – that Liu is a criminal serving his sentence and the award is a challenge to China's legal system. But have a look at the verdict in Liu's case and you will see his crime is nothing more than his writing, and drafting the 08 Charter – a clear admission that his imprisonment breaches international principles. Why only call him a criminal, and not mention what he did to become one? But I cannot blame the staff of the Ministry of Foreign Affairs for their stupidity – what else can they do?

Today is Human Rights Day, and the Nobel Peace Prize will be awarded in Oslo. The Chinese government and its people are normally remarkably fond of international awards. Xi Haifeng became an overnight national hero after winning China's first ever gold at the 1984 Los Angeles Olympics. China's female volleyball team won five major titles from 1981 to 1986 and created a political slogan as well as a sporting success story – we were exhorted to embody the 'Female Volleyball Team Spirit'. The Asian Games, the Olympic Games, the World Expo – these are all just games or exhibitions, but the government uses them to unite the nation. Yet one of us wins a Nobel Prize and the authorities panic. The winner is not someone they like – he is a critic of the government, someone they have thrown in jail.

The Nobel ceremony will still go ahead regardless, but an arrogant and disgraced government still intends to save some face. Hence the lies and violence, plots and farce. Many have been put under house arrest, or taken 'for a holiday'. Others have policemen standing outside their homes watching their every move. Internet and phone lines have been cut. Others have simply disappeared. Never mind international travel, we are not even free in China, in our own homes. Is this the rule of law? Are these Chinese-style human rights?

But silencing voices of opposition is more important than any other task, particularly in the age of the internet. Many know Liu Xiaobo has won the Nobel Peace Prize and are spreading the good news. The more the authorities clamp down, the more the public wants to know the truth. The empty chair at the ceremony shames our weak rulers and can only make them the butt of jokes.

So on Human Rights Day, I fast. For Liu Xianbin, for Liu Xiaobo, and for the future of China. It may do no good, but I express the wishes of one watched and oppressed citizen. The state security police just phoned saying I must see them. I have put them off till the afternoon. I want to share how I feel and what I believe with those on both sides of China's walls. Remain alert, alert to the harm that is done in your name. We may not be able to resist, but we must never forget to tell them of our anger! ◻

First published in Chinese on Chinaeweekly.com, 19 December 2010

©Chen Wei
41(1): 107/112
DOI: 10.1177/0306422012438818
www.indexoncensorship.org

manifestos for the 21st century

EDITED BY URSULA OWEN AND JUDITH VIDAL-HALL

Whose Liberty is it Anyway?

EUROPE AT THE CROSSROADS

STEFAN AUER

MAY 2012, PB, 120PP, \$9.50 / £6

ISBN 978 0 8574 2 040 4

Europe's turn of fortune is humbling, humiliating and, perhaps, irreversible. What went wrong, and when? Old questions have now acquired new meaning: Is it possible to maintain conditions for self-government while undermining the nation-state? What are the limits of solidarity? Can Europe be truly united through its common history, or its common currency? Is further unity in Europe even desirable?

Beyond the Wall

WRITING A PATH THROUGH PALESTINE

BIDISHA

MAY 2012, PB, 124PP, \$9.50 / £6

ISBN 978 0 8574 2 039 8

Their voices come from Bethlehem and Hebron. You can hear them from Jerusalem to Nazareth, and witness their protests in Gaza and Ramallah. From the refugee camps in the West Bank, you can hear the voices of the Palestinian people call out to demand self-determination and a better quality of life. But outside of Israel and the occupied territories, these individual voices are rarely heard—until now.

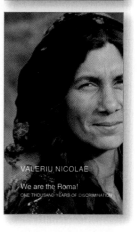

We are the Roma!

ONE THOUSAND YEARS OF DISCRIMINATION

VALERIU NICOLAE

MAY 2012, PB, 120PP, \$9.50 / £6

ISBN 978 0 8574 2 038 1

The violent discrimination and ghettoization of Roma communities continue today inside the EU despite legislation designed to protect them against racism.no country or official body has taken up the case of the Roma and strongly argued for their protection and integration.Valeriu Nicolae, himself a Romanian Roma, gives voice to the Roma cause, offering a precise and candid look at their current situation.

LONDON NEW YORK CALCUTTA
www.seagullbooks.org

TRADE ENQUIRIES TO UPM, 0117 9020275
DISTRIBUTED BY JOHN WILEY, 1243 779777
FOR THE UNIVERSITY OF CHICAGO PRESS
www.press.uchicago.edu

RIGHTS ONLINE

Rebecca MacKinnon

In the United States, under two successive administrations of both parties, laws have been passed, policies implemented and corporate practices evolved that make it much easier for government agencies to track and access citizens' private digital communications – stored 'in the cloud' on corporate servers or transmitted through privately operated internet and wireless services – than it is for agents to search or carry out surveillance of our physical homes, offices, vehicles and mail.

In the internet age, it is inevitable that corporations and government agencies will have access to detailed information about people's lives. We willingly share personal information with companies for the convenience of using their products. We accept that a certain amount of surveillance is necessary in order to protect innocent people from crime and terror. But Americans have failed to address the resulting dilemma: how do we prevent the abuse of power that we have willingly delegated to government and companies in exchange for security and convenience?

Answering this question is critical not only for the future of American democracy but for democracy and human rights around the world as people everywhere – from Tahrir Square to Zuccotti Park – grow ever more dependent on the internet and mobile phones for organising protests and demanding political change. An important first step is the commitment by everyone who exercises power on and through the internet to respect and uphold the human rights of internet users.

National commitment: Civil liberties, human rights and privacy organisations should be included in the process of drafting all legislation, involving internet regulation, from an early stage. Laws that empower the executive branch to access citizens' private communications or restrict access to information without sufficient legislative and judicial oversight should be revised.

Diplomatic commitment: Democratic governments should make a clear commitment to uphold internet users' free expression and privacy rights in their trade, intellectual property and law enforcement treaties. Oversight mechanisms should be created with the heavy involvement of global civil society.

Corporate commitment: All companies in the information communications technology (ICT) sector should commit to uphold basic principles of free expression and privacy for their users, and agree to be held independently accountable to their commitments. They can most easily do both of these things by joining the Global Network Initiative, a multi-stakeholder initiative dedicated to promoting core standards of free expression and privacy in the ICT sector.

Shared commitment to transparency and accountability: All companies should be required to report regularly and publicly on how content is deleted or blocked, under what circumstances and at whose behest. Companies should also be required to report publicly and clearly on how they gather and retain user information, and how they share that information both with government and other companies.

Public commitment to engagement and vigilance: Citizens of democracies need to understand that the internet is a politically contested space. We need to pay attention to who is exerting power on our digital lives and fight to defend our rights just as many of us have grown accustomed to doing in our physical towns, cities and nations. That means we should exercise our voice and our power as customers and users, to push companies whose services we depend on to respect our rights. As investors, we can choose to support those parts of the industry which are making clear commitments and efforts to support free expression and privacy. As voters, we must make clear to our elected representatives that we are watching them, and will punish them at the ballot box if they pass laws that could constrict our right to free expression and assembly online.

Whether the internet evolves in a manner that is compatible with democracy in the long run is not pre-determined. It depends on the choices and actions of millions of internet users, along with the engineers, programmers and legislators who shape what people can or cannot do in cyberspace. It is time for the world's democracies at least – and their citizens – to make and demand core commitments to human rights on the internet. ❏

©Rebecca MacKinnon
41(1): 114/115
DOI: 10.1177/0306422012439660
www.indexoncensorship.org

Rebecca MacKinnon is the author of *Consent of the Networked* (Basic Books). She is a co-founder of Global Voices and a member of *Index*'s advisory board

LOST IMAGES

Zeina Aboul Hosn's interviews with activists were seized in a raid on her flat in Damascus. She laments the loss in a candid letter to the Syrian secret police

To the Man Who Took the Footage We Had Filmed During a Month Working Undercover in Syria, as well as My Journal, and My Laptop

I don't know anything about you. I have a mental image of you, a stereotype in a cheap fake leather jacket and a dark moustache. I imagine you searching the flat, throwing clothes and bed-sheets around, ripping beads off necklaces, tearing open tampons and packets of painkillers, grabbing the camera, the hard drives, my laptop, my journal. Smiling to yourself at your cleverness and your accomplishment. You didn't expect to find so much so easily, did you?

I don't know if you were following us from the start or if you just stumbled upon us that day. It was our last day in Damascus. How ironic. Or maybe not.

Did you laugh at our stupidity, leaving everything in the same flat we used to live in and eat in and interview wanted opposition activists? Don't shit where you eat. Or deal with the consequences.

There was a half-hearted attempt at heightened security I must admit. We hid the hard drive in the washing machine. Just the once. It felt silly.

Stupid. No one could possibly come and search the flat. These things just don't happen. You hear about them, but they don't really happen to us. The Mukhabarat, the secret police, do not raid my bedroom and take my journal and my laptop – these things don't happen in my real life.

Anyway. That is how I imagine you. With an arrogant grin and a bag full of the Mukhabarat equivalent of finding a bag of pills in the grass on the last day of a festival. The fun has just begun.

Do you count on the arrogance of undercover filmmakers? Do you count on the blindness of those immersed in a film? Do you count on the liberties we take, on the mistakes we make? Sit back and relax. Let us do your work for you. Let us deliver you their necks in the noose. Let me write and sign my own confession while I have my morning cup of coffee.

The last thing my mother said to me before I left for Damascus was 'never trust a Syrian'.

To be frank, I have always had a strained relationship with Syria, ranging between love, hate and paranoia. My first memory of Syria is of the border at night. I am in the car with my parents and brother and sister. It is very very dark. We are trying to cross into Lebanon but the officers at the border want bribes – they take our bread, some rotten bananas, perfume, my mother's jewellery. They terrified me. And in Lebanon we always lived in the shadow of this invisible evil presence: the Mukhabarat.

They are always out to get you, and they know EVERYTHING. It's like CCTV with fangs and handcuffs and bad haircuts. We grew up hearing stories. Of people disappearing, of torture, of surveillance, of corruption and bribery.

Do you count on the liberties we take or the mistakes we make?

But I never thought we would get so close, you and I. I never thought our paths would cross.

Close, and yet total strangers. You know so much about me. Would you recognise me if you saw me in the street? Or perhaps if you heard my thoughts?

Have I ever seen you? Were you ever sat next to me in the bar? Did you walk past me in the street? Did I brush past you as I bought some bread at the corner shop?

It's crazy how the mind starts spinning these fantasy scenes and images, made up of a steady diet of nothing except paranoia and hearsay. You leave me with no proof either way. My faceless foe.

You took my friend. You took my work.

You have shaken my faith in what I do.

You did your job. I congratulate you. A worthy opponent.

You did your job. I did not do mine.

At the end of the day, we are all just trying to get by.

I came, I saw, I filmed, I left behind a trail of imprisoned activists, families smuggled into safety in other countries, people still living in fear of being caught.

Never trust a Syrian. Never trust a filmmaker. ❐

©Zeina Aboul Hosn
41(1): 116/118
DOI: 10.1177/0306422012439381
www.indexoncensorship.org

Zeina Aboul Hosn is a Lebanese documentary filmmaker

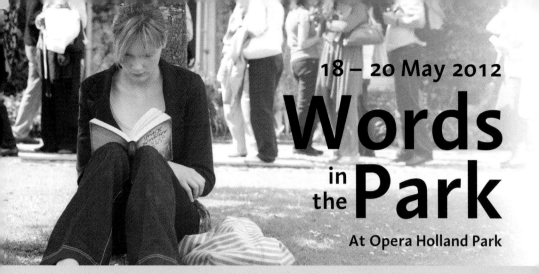

18 – 20 May 2012

Words

in the Park

At Opera Holland Park

A three-day literature festival in Holland Park, London

his spring ideas, creativity and debate will be in bloom as Ways With Vords gathers together a world-class line-up for a brand new festival.

riday 18 May

1.00 **John McCarthy & Sandi Toksvig**
alestine and Beyond

2.45 **Sophie Dahl & Mary McCartney**
ood Glorious Food

.30 **Maureen Lipman**
Must Collect Myself

.15 **Mary Quant**
igh Priestess of
ixties Fashion

.00 **A.S. Byatt**
n conversation with
he *New Statesman*

.45 **Google Key Note Debate**
nternet: Breaking
Down the Barriers of
stablishment

Saturday 19 May

11.00 **Jeremy Paxman**
What Empire did
for Britain

12.45 **Bettany Hughes**
Socrates
and the Good Life

2.30 **Gavin Pretor-Pinney**
Looking at Clouds

4.15 **Alain de Botton**
Religion for Atheists

6.00 **Jung Chang**
Wild Swans: 21 Years On

Sunday 20 May

11.00 **A.A. Gill**
Globe Trotter

12.45 **Evan Davis**
How Britain
Earns its Living

2.30 **P.D. James & Penelope Lively**
Writers' Lives

4.15 **Tony Benn & Owen Jones**
Looking to the Future

6.00 **Andrew Marr**
Elizabeth II:
A Life Examined

Tickets £12 (Day Tickets £50)
from OHP box office: **0300 999 1000**
Events last 1 hour   Booking opens 10 April.
Refreshments and book signings will be available
throughout the festival.
For full programme details visit
www.wayswithwords.co.uk

Official Bookseller
Waterstones
Online Partner
Google

Middle East

Naji al-Ali

Cartoons

From Lebanon to Kuwait, the cartoonist has so far survived attempts to stop his work.

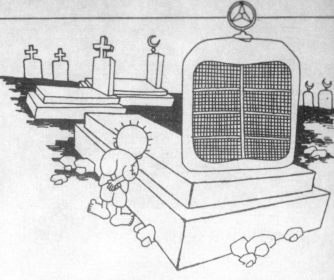

Introducing Cartoons For Amnesty, *Art Buchwald wrote 'The political cartoon has been one of the most powerful weapons through the ages. . . . Dictators of the right and the left fear the political cartoonist more than they do the atomic bomb. No totalitarian government can afford to be ridiculed.'*

In the Middle East where words are closely scrutinised by the state, the humour that a cartoon provides has become an important outlet for political criticism. Strict censorship, and high illiteracy rates, have helped Naji al-Ali achieve the big success he now enjoys throughout the region despite the official weight he still incurs in every country of the Middle East to varying degrees.

Naji al-Ali uses his pen as a tool to fight the very things that account for his success. Having much freedom of expression and freedom of political choice his cause throughout the Arab world, he fights not with word but with drawing off the inconsistencies in his justice that suffer from lack of democracy. The message his cartoons carry in the Arab world were yet but too visible; he was deported from more than one country in the Middle East, and he also has various jails.

Lately, following the rising tension in the area, a few political and social groups in various countries of the Middle East have issued governments to 'censoring' al-Ali, threatening physical violence and burning and destroying newspaper offices. He still draws but always is moves that

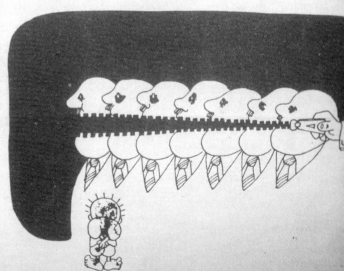

al-Ali continues to prosper, and with him the art of caricature as a new medium to ward off the censor. *Ghalia Qabani, a Syrian journalist, interviewed al-Ali for* Index on Censorship.

Naji is not quite sure of the year of his birth. But he was born in Shajara, a small village that lies between Nazra and Tiberias. In 1948 the family had to leave their home and settled in the Ein al-Helwa refugee camp in south Lebanon.

GHALIA QABANI How did you discover your talent?

NAJI AL-ALI As soon as I was aware of what was going on, all the havoc in our region, I felt I had to do something, to contribute somehow. First, I tried politics, to join a party, I marched in demonstrations, but it was not really me. The thing was I felt

within me needed a different m express what I was going throug some time in the fifties that I starte on the walls of our camp. Du period, the refugees had begun to some political awareness as a re what had been taking place in the revolution in Egypt, a war of inde in Algeria, things were brewing i the Arab world. My job, I felt, wa up for those people, my people in the camps, in Egypt, in Algeria, th Arabs all over the region who ha outlets to express their power of my job to voice them, for the of a political conviction, to h provide a new means for f

POWERFUL WEAPONS

By placing ordinary Arabs at the centre of his work, fearless cartoonist **Naji al Ali** spoke volumes about life in the Middle East

Art Buchwald wrote: 'The political cartoon has been one of the most powerful weapons through the ages ... Dictators of the right and the left fear the political cartoonist more than they do the atomic bomb. No totalitarian government can afford to be ridiculed.'

In the Middle East, where words are closely scrutinised by the state, the humour that a cartoon provides has become an important outlet for political criticism. Strict censorship and high illiteracy rates have helped Naji al Ali achieve the big success he now enjoys throughout the region despite the official wrath he still incurs in every country of the Middle East in varying degrees.

Naji al Ali uses his pen as a tool to fight the very things that account for his success. Having made freedom of expression and freedom of political choice his cause throughout the Arab world, he fights not with words but with drawings all the institutions in his society that suffer from lack of democracy. The message his cartoons carry to the Arab reader soon got him into trouble: he was deported from more than one country in the Middle East, and he also lost various jobs.

Lately, following the rising tension in the area, a few political and social groups in various countries of the Middle East have joined governments in condemning al Ali, threatening physical violence and making other intimidating statements against the artist. Despite these attempts to muzzle him, al Ali continues to prosper, and with him the art of caricature as a new medium to ward off the censor. Ghalia Qabani, a Syrian journalist, interviewed al Ali for *Index on Censorship*.

Naji is not quite sure of the year of his birth. But he was born in Shajara, a small village that lies between Nazareth and Tiberias. In 1948 the family had to leave their home and settled in the Ein el Hilweh refugee camp in south Lebanon.

Ghalia Qabani: How did you discover your talent?

Naji al Ali: As soon as I was aware of what was going on, all the havoc in our region, I felt I had to do something, to contribute somehow. First, I tried politics, to join a party, I marched in demonstrations, but that was not really me. The sharp cries I felt within me needed a different medium to express what I was going through. It was some time in the 50s that I started drawing on the walls of our camp. During that period, the refugees had begun to develop some political awareness as a reaction to what had been taking place in the region: a revolution in Egypt, a war of independence in Algeria, things were brewing all around the Arab world. My job, I felt, was to speak up for those people, my people who are in the camps, in Egypt, in Algeria, the simple Arabs all over the region who have very few outlets to express their points of view. I felt my job was to incite them. For the function of a political cartoonist, as I see it, is to provide a new vision. He is a missionary, in a sense, because it is just a little bit harder to censor a cartoon than an article.

Ghalia Qabani: How did all that evolve into a profession?

Naji al Ali: I started to use drawing as a form of political expression in Lebanese jails. I was detained by the Deuxieme Bureau [the Lebanese intelligence service] as a result of the measures the Bureau was undertaking to contain political activities in the Palestinian camps during the 60s. I drew on the prison walls and subsequently Ghassan Kanafani, a journalist and publisher of *al Huria* magazine [assassinated in Beirut in 1971], saw some of those drawings and encouraged me to continue, and eventually published some of my cartoons. Later I fled to Kuwait. The margin of freedom and democracy that exists in Kuwait enabled me to grow. There my cartoons concentrated on the dangers surrounding us as people.

My job, I felt, was to speak up for people, in the camps, in the region

Ghalia Qabani: What about your work in Beirut?

Naji al Ali: Working for *al Safir* newspaper in Beirut in 1971 was the best part of my life, and the most productive. There, surrounded by the violence of many an army and finally by the Israeli invasion, I stood facing it all with my pen every day. I never felt fear, failure or despair, and I didn't surrender. I faced armies with cartoons: with drawings of flowers, hope and bullets. Yes, hope is essential, always. My work in Beirut made me once again closer to the refugees in the camps, the poor and the harassed.

Ghalia Qabani: 'Hanzala', that little boy who stands in every one of your cartoons with his hands crossed behind his back as if he were a spectator at a continuing show, when and where was he born?

Naji al Ali: This child, as you can see, is neither beautiful, spoilt, nor even well-fed. He is barefoot like many children in refugee camps. He is actually ugly and no woman would wish to have a child like him. However, those who came to know 'Hanzala', as I discovered later, loved him and later adopted him because he is affectionate, honest, outspoken, and a bum. He is an icon that stands to watch me from slipping. And his hands behind his back are a symbol of rejection of all the present negative tides in our region. I have to admit also that as a child I was fascinated by the theatre. I loved it a lot. I had dreams of appearing on stage, communicating with people. Lately, I have discovered that my love for the theatre is still very much alive and, in fact, my cartoons are a form of theatre. That space in the newspaper is the stage that I appear on every morning. Yes, I reach out for and communicate with an audience every day without troubling them to come to me, as if I were on stage. When I found that out I felt a sense of peace and balance within me.

Ghalia Qabani: How do you deal with having a family, having to move house so many times, and having to draw every day?

Naji al Ali: My wife Widad is just the opposite of everything I am. She is an organised, logical person while I am disorganised, my thoughts scattered in every direction. So, you see, we complement each other perfectly. She has become my safety valve. She watches over my moods and any changes that could indicate I am beginning to forget or have ambitions at the expense of the truth. Yet she never interferes or tries to warn me of the dangers of being too outspoken.

Ghalia Qabani: What about the Palestinians? Many would like to censor your cartoons for you often criticise their behaviour ...

Naji al Ali: I draw Palestinians as I see them. I draw Palestinian political figures, and I think it is essential for any leadership to accept criticism. I also draw rich Palestinians who scream all day about the land and about sacrifices when in fact they

are more interested in their financial deals and private gains. I criticise Palestinian women who were farmers a few years back and have now turned into city ladies living in Canada and Brazil.

Ghalia Qabani: Does the continuous deterioration of civil liberties in the Middle East give you a sense of despair?

Naji al Ali: When I was younger I thought I would actually be able to help achieve all our aspirations for independence, unity, justice. Many died for those aspirations and things are only getting worse. That, certainly, can make one despair. But, more than ever, I feel a sense of duty to go on doing what I have to and can do. ❏

©Naji al Ali
41(1): 120/125
DOI: 10.1177/0306422012438659
www.indexoncensorship.org

Naji al Ali was born in Palestine. One of the Middle East's most celebrated political cartoonists, he was assassinated in London on 22 July 1987. This article first appeared in *Index on Censorship* Volume 13, Number 6, December 1984

Credit: Naji al Ali

NEW TACTICS

Christopher Soghoian

In 2011 the surveillance industry was exposed. Investigative journalists, aided by documents obtained from the offices of state security agencies in post-revolution Egypt and Libya, revealed the western firms that had provided surveillance technologies to those governments. Similarly, large caches of surveillance product marketing materials were released by WikiLeaks, Privacy International and the *Wall Street Journal*. These 'spy files' detail the advanced capabilities of censorship and surveillance products, sold to governments around the world, that make up the $5bn annual trade.

Following these disclosures, Secretary of State Hillary Clinton publicly condemned the 'companies selling the hardware and software of repression to authoritarian governments'. Similarly, Republican Congressman Chris Smith reintroduced the Global Online Freedom Act, now tweaked to regulate the sale of censorship and surveillance technology. Although well intentioned, the bill has little chance of passing.

Politicians voice concerns about the largely unregulated market for this technology in humanitarian terms: the governments of Egypt, Syria and Iran are spying on human rights activists, journalists and dissidents, who are then arrested, beaten or killed. However, given the neverending list of serious human rights problems, it is unsurprising that many politicians seem unwilling to invest the political capital to address this issue. After all, Egyptian activists do not vote in Texas (nor London for that matter).

The problem is this: as long as the trade in surveillance technology is framed as a human rights issue, it will compete for the attention of politicians and the general public. This approach is doomed to failure. Instead, activists should reframe the debate by focusing on national security, something that no post-9/11 politician can afford to ignore.

Although governments spy on their own citizens, they also spy on foreigners. However, the snooping technology that is used abroad is very different. This is because intelligence agencies are unlikely to receive the same kind of helpful assistance that they have come to expect from phone companies when they engage in foreign surveillance. As an example, while AT&T has gone out of its way to help the US National Security Agency, the phone company is of little use when the Americans wish to spy on Chinese domestic communications.

One of the most effective ways for intelligence agencies to intercept communications in a foreign country is to use 'IMSI catchers', which are briefcase-sized snooping devices that mimic the signals broadcast by normal mobile phone towers. When one of these devices is turned on, all nearby phones will connect to it, as it will appear to be a legitimate phone tower. The IMSI catchers can then be used to track and locate particular phones, or to intercept calls, text messages and data connections.

IMSI catchers are available from surveillance vendors around the world, are easy to transport, and are difficult to detect when used. It is also likely that they have been sold to countries that have a history of engaging in foreign espionage against the United States and other western governments.

Our governments have long been willing to ignore – or in some cases promote – the sale of surveillance technologies to authoritarian regimes. However, once IMSI catchers have been sold to the governments of Russia, Pakistan and China, there is no way of guaranteeing that they will only be used in Moscow, Lahore or Beijing. After all, the technology does not require the assistance of the local phone company and therefore works equally well in Washington.

Although the privacy threat posed by IMSI catchers is not widely known to the general public, it is real. Furthermore, as these devices have been purchased by intelligence agencies, they are likely used to spy on the traditional targets of foreign espionage: politicians, military leaders and business executives. For advocates, then, IMSI catchers and other surveillance technologies that can be used for foreign espionage are a fantastic opportunity. We must shift the debate away from human rights to national security, and in particular to the threat posed by such technologies when they are used by foreign governments in our own capital cities. Only then will our leaders find the will power to regulate the global trade in surveillance technology seriously. ❐

©Christopher Soghoian
41(1): 126/127
DOI: 10.1177/0306422012438319
www.indexoncensorship.org

Christopher Soghoian is a privacy and security researcher based in Washington, DC

SHADOW OF DISSENT

The murder of Hrant Dink remains a trauma for Turkish society. Five years on, **Kaya Genç** talks to some of Turkey's bravest voices about speaking out

During a dramatically snowy week in Istanbul last January, the trial of Hrant Dink, the Turkish-Armenian journalist who was assassinated in 2007, came to an awkward and unsatisfying conclusion. Two men directly involved with the murder were convicted, but no acknowledgement was made of the political forces that organised and made possible such a masterfully executed killing. A few days after the verdict, more than 40,000 people marched from Istanbul's Taksim Square to the offices of Dink's newspaper *Agos*, to commemorate the fifth anniversary of his death. The march quickly turned into a political meeting as thousands of people protested the verdict, chanting the slogan: 'This is not over until we say so.' For the protesters who marched on that cold January day, those convicted were no more than the tip of the iceberg. The crowd demanded the government investigate the case further, with the firm belief that a more sinister and complex story was still to be uncovered.

When I decided to talk to Turkish dissidents to gain a deeper understanding of the tragic fate of many intellectuals in the country, two images haunted me: the ceaseless snow and the shadow of Dink's murder. A week before the protests, I met Murat Belge, a professor of comparative literature,

who is considered to be among Turkey's leading dissidents. Five years ago he had stood on the pavement where his friend Dink had just been murdered. The sight of the tens of thousands of people who quickly gathered that night to protest the killing shocked but also partly reassured him. He told me how he had never expected such a reaction, but that it at least gave him something to be proud of on that ominous day.

Belge has been studying Turkish society for a long time. Four decades ago, he founded the monthly political magazine *Birikim*, which introduced the ideas of the French theorist Louis Althusser to Turkish socialists and played a decisive role in influencing many Turkish communists to become dissidents of the regime. Belge is also the publisher of Orhan Pamuk, Turkey's Nobel Laureate, who shares a similarly scrutinising view of the authoritative tendencies in Turkish culture.

Belge played a formative role during my own university years. As a lecturer on Romantic poetry, he taught me iambic pentameter, along with the Lake Poets and the political responsibilities that come with being a dissenting writer.

An influential political commentator, he also happens to be the Turkish translator of James Joyce's *A Portrait of the Artist as a Young Man*. With his long beard and wisely smiling eyes, Belge physically resembles Joyce's similarly witty and passionate compatriot George Bernard Shaw.

During the 1970s, Belge worked as an assistant in the English department of Istanbul University while also participating in the political activities of a radical leftist group. The department of English played a decisive role in his life and was founded in 1939 by Halide Edip Adıvar, a major novelist, English scholar and dissident of the Republican era, later denounced as a traitor by the regime for her criticisms of its authoritarian practices. Located in Turkey's oldest university, the literature department also prides itself for having provided a safe haven to Eric Auerbach, the founder of the discipline of comparative literature, during the Nazi era.

After the military coup of 1971, Belge was arrested for his political activities. He was tortured and jailed for two years. Long afterwards, in an interview, he identified among his torturers a Turkish general, who is

Demonstrators hold banners reading 'We all are Hrant, we are all Armenian'
after an Istanbul court rejects allegations that Dink's murder was the result of an
organised conspiracy. It is also the anniversary of Dink's murder, 19 January 2012
Credit: EPA/Alamy

currently serving a prison sentence for his role in the political group Ergenekon which allegedly planned the assassinations of high-profile dissidents, including Hrant Dink. Belge was held in the notorious Ziverbey Kiosk in Kadıköy where high-ranking generals interrogated and tortured those they considered enemies of the Turkish state.

A decade later, when Belge was an assistant professor of English literature in Istanbul University, he was forced to resign from his tenure following the 1980 coup. Those were the Kenan Evren years, named after the general who pledged to put an end to what he saw as the chaos caused by Turkish dissidents. All political activities were outlawed by the generals and Turkish socialists were forced once again to go underground. In a seminal essay published in the *New Left Review*, 'The Tragedy of the Turkish Left', Belge gave an account of how Turkish socialists dealt with the issue of political violence – of which they were victims during the coups. He came to the conclusion that, for various sections of the left, 'the question of power became an obsession' and 'the fetishisation of "immediate" power and "total" struggle drew the left further and further away from reality'. The left, in other words, was forced to be forceful, pushed towards authoritarianism by the regime.

When I met him to discuss the situation of Turkish dissidents today, Belge seemed to have retained this perspective. I could instantly see that his outlook as an intellectual was deeply suspicious of militant forms of socialism. My impression was confirmed when Belge made a practical distinction between a political opponent and a dissident. The former merely seeks to have a grip on power, he argued, while the latter struggles to undermine and deconstruct it. For most of his life, Belge's sympathies have lain with the latter; he believes that the regime perceived dissidents as the greater threat and that was among the reasons they were singled out.

As we walked towards a restaurant in the university campus where we planned to conduct the interview, a young student wearing a headscarf approached Belge and asked a question about her exam results. Moments

Mexico – 2006

As attacks against journalists increase and impunity becomes the norm, the body of Misael Tamayo Hernández is found in November with his hands tied behind his back. Tamayo owned and edited newspaper *El Despertar de la Costa*, which regularly reported on corruption.

later, a gay activist invited him to a meeting. As a long-time supporter of freedom of expression and human rights, Belge seems to be a favourite with political student groups. The usual custom in Turkey is to show solidarity with one's own political allies, but Belge plays a different game. In his adamant support for the rights of conservatives, progressives and ethnic minorities alike, he has made friends across Turkish society with those who feel wronged and oppressed by the regime. And ironically, once added together, the marginalised may even prove to be a majority rather than a minority in the country.

Belge emphasises the importance of being a dissident rather than a mere opponent to the regime and illustrated his point. 'Think of an oil well,' he says. 'Two groups of men approach it. We have those who follow the ruler and those who follow his opponent. Both discuss but fail to come to an agreement on the best method to drill the largest possible amount of oil from the well. And then another character appears and asks them: "Hey guys, why do we need this oil in the first place? Why don't we give up on drilling entirely and look for alternative sources of energy instead?"'

The usual custom is to show solidarity with one's own allies

Belge has asked similarly fundamental questions during his career as a lecturer and publisher. Now in his 60s, his findings can scarcely be said to be optimistic. 'The sad fact is that there has never been dissidence in Turkey,' he says. 'When I look at the so-called opponents of the government, they fail to convince me that there will indeed be a significant difference when they exercise power themselves.' To illustrate his argument, he pointed to how almost nobody struggled against the industrialisation process which accompanied the foundation of the Turkish Republic. Industrialisation meant power and authority and everyone wanted to be a part of this new phenomenon, which made any form of dissent intolerable. 'Never did we have intellectuals like Gandhi in this country,' Belge says, 'whereas a profound analysis of the industrialisation process would actually prove crucial for the left to redefine itself.' The first wave of Turkish dissidents included figures such as Adıvar and Mustafa Suphi, the latter being the leader of Turkish communists. He later

drowned in the Black Sea alongside his comrades in what many believed to be a massacre organised by the regime. Belge acknowledges Suphi's assassination as one of the earliest cases of its kind in Turkey. He also points to how, after the massacre of communists whose sympathies lay with the Soviets, the founders of the Republic quickly pulled significant names from the left inside the tent to avoid the emergence of an independent popular movement: the founder of the Republic, Mustafa Kemal Atatürk, had asked the communists to work within the frame of the state rather than allying with the Soviets. As a result, many leftists quickly came to an agreement with the regime and gathered around the influential *Kadro* magazine, channelling their dissent into a statist movement instead. Belge's own father, Burhan Belge, was one of those young men whose early socialist ideals were sacrificed for an administrative position in the government. He, and others who made the same compromise, then had to accept the hegemony of the one-party regime. Many intellectuals who had been in opposition during the first three decades of the Turkish Republic now found themselves in the similarly uncomfortable position of being allies of the state or at best toothless opponents. Belge believes that both groups were obsessed with grasping the political power of the Turkish state.

During the 1980s, Belge became one of the leading figures on the Turkish left. When Polish general Wojciech Jaruzelski imposed martial law in Poland in 1981, Belge compared the militarist character of his regime to the Turkish coup of 1980. Both coups aimed to defend a regime the generals feared was undermined by its people. 'I was working for a leftist newspaper at the time,' Belge says. 'The editors, like many leftists in the country, secretly supported Jaruzelski's rule; in fact they secretly supported the Turkish coup as well, believing the generals had saved their regimes from destruction. In the beginning, the US administration supported the Turkish military, but when it later criticised its human rights abuses, the general staff took an anti-US stance and started talking about sovereignty and national values. Many leftists who secretly supported the military now openly embraced its anti-US stance for that was precisely the thing they understood from the word "socialism": an armed opposition to the US.' This resembled what Belge in his *New Left Review* piece called the 'tragedy' of the Turkish left: a vicious circle that not only destroys its political enemies but also manages to recreate them in its own image.

Belge first met Hrant Dink in 1993 during a conference of the Helsinki Citizens' Assembly, a non-governmental organisation working for human rights and pluralism, whose Turkish branch Belge had founded in the early 1990s. When I asked about his initial impressions of Dink, Belge characterised him as an affectionate, passionate intellectual who was uncomfortable with mainstream politics. Belge believes that Dink's pacifist, anti-mainstream stance was among the reasons that led to his assassination. 'Let me give you an example,' he said. 'Before his assassination, we visited Yerevan together. I remember coming across a statue of an ancient Armenian military commander. I asked him who he was. "He has a sword, don't you see, don't you understand?" Dink replied. "When you are ready to kill someone, when you have a *sword* in your hand, it is enough for them to erect a statue of you."

'This was the perspective for which he was murdered. The state apparatus has in fact no problem with Armenian hardliners. If you have a nationalist agenda, be it Turkish or Armenian, that position is acceptable in the sense that it is politically clear. But if you are a dissenter, like Dink was, then they can't place you anywhere. I believe that when they killed him, they killed "love"', he says with a grieving voice. 'Love is not an easy thing to get rid of so they killed Dink instead for he represented exactly that: a form of love and affection.'

In 2008, Belge was among those who organised an academic conference about Armenians in the Ottoman period, where Dink gave a moving speech about how deeply-rooted Turkish Armenians had always been in Turkey. 'People were so afraid about the whole conference,' Belge says. 'They thought if we discussed the Armenian issue in Turkey there would be a catastrophe. But nothing of the sort happened. Swallows continued to fly, flowers were still blossoming and rivers floated peacefully by.'

I was reminded of these words when, as I left Belge that evening, a large flock of swallows flew above me and disappeared into the black night. The next day they were nowhere to be seen. It was a brighter day but still freezing. I hopped onto a ferry to reach Kadıköy, a neighbourhood located on İstanbul's Anatolian side. During a windy trip I stayed indoors, looking at a children's book, *The Nocturnal Sun*, and a young adult novel, *When The Moon Meets the Sea*, both written by Karin Karakaşlı, a young Turkish-Armenian author and translator whose life changed dramatically when she met Hrant Dink more than a decade ago. After editing the culture section of

Burma – 2007

Pro-democracy protesters take to the streets in Rangoon, many of them led by Buddhist monks. Hundreds are detained and attacked during the crackdown that follows.

Dink's newspaper *Agos* for many years, she is now a lecturer in the university as well as a prolific writer.

Karakaşlı is fluent in Armenian, German, English and Turkish. One of the most interesting figures to emerge in a new wave of Turkish writers who define themselves as political dissidents, I first met her at a Winternachten meeting three years ago, where we both participated in a discussion about the politics of fiction. I remember how she gave a touching speech about the moment she heard of the death of her dear friend; knowing the sensitivity of the issue, I decided not to mention the name of Dink during our interview. But as I met her in a Kadıköy cafe overlooking the Bosphorus, Dink's figure clearly cast a shadow over us and, without mentioning his name, we gradually became aware that we were, in a sense, talking about his legacy.

Hrant is not a court case. He is an unclosed wound

During the 1980s, Karakaşlı was a great fan of children's books, including Hans Christian Andersen's tales. When she wrote a children's book herself almost three decades later, she understood that it was all about creating a sense of justice, a concept that had long been a central issue for her after witnessing many injustices committed against those perceived to be on the margins: 'Children's books are never innocent,' Karakaşlı told me. 'In fact they are dangerous in the sense that they raise fundamental questions about the origins of things. If they stop asking questions and become didactic, then the careful look of the child immediately perceives the bossy tone and loses interest. Therefore writing a book for a younger audience proved to be an extremely edifying process for me.'

Karakaşlı has a rare position as a writer who inhabits four languages and four cultures. 'German has a privileged place for me,' she said. 'It is a culture that I find very distant, but that distance proved to have a liberating effect on me. I love Berlin for the same reasons. There is a bit of everything there and nobody judges you for who you are. To be able to have such a hybrid culture in the land of the so-called "Aryan race" is without a doubt an immense historical irony.'

The multiculturalism she described sounded fine, but what about Turkey? From her answer I could understand how she found it very difficult to agree with the politics of the mainstream parties. Karakaşlı has little sympathy for the main opposition party CHP, the Republican People's Party, which regularly denies any historical wrongdoing during the early years of the Republic. But she is also worried by the political manoeuvres of Prime Minister Recep Tayyip Erdoğan and his ruling party, even though they publicly apologised for the massacres of Turkey's Kurdish population in the 1930s. Karakaşlı told me how she was irritated by the use of history for political ends. The latest furore in the media, following the French Senate's passing of a law that made the denial of the Armenian genocide a crime for French citizens, created a very uncomfortable atmosphere in Turkey, as was expected. The nationalist sentiment was once again on the rise and the discourse of the main political parties became extremely defensive towards historical issues. For all those reasons Karakaşlı considers her politics to be outside the mainstream. 'During last year's elections, for example, every choice seemed equally false to me,' she says.

Karakaşlı works for an Armenian high school where she teaches Armenian to a class of 17 year olds. I asked her to describe her students' responses to the public discussion of Turkish-Armenian issues. 'These students possess a special ethnic background and they dislike prejudices,' she said. 'Some way or other, they are wounded by what they read in history books which are infamous for their presentation of Turkish Armenians as no better than a bunch of enemies and traitors.'

During the time Karakaşlı worked for *Agos* newspaper, Hrant Dink was accused of insulting Turkishness in one of his articles, a crime under the infamous Article 301 of the Turkish penal code. Even though she was associated with the case primarily through her responsibility as an editor, the event had a lasting impact: the trial was used to present Dink as a traitor to the country. When I asked her about whether the authorities still intimidate *Agos* with threats of prosecution, she pointed to how the very survival of Article 301 was a sign of the ongoing limitations. 'Sarkis Saropyan, an editor of *Agos*, was condemned to one year in prison alongside Hrant's son, Arat Dink,' she says. 'And that verdict came *after* Dink was murdered.' She also described Turkish dissidents' concerns at a speech given last December by the current Interior Minister Idris Sahin in which he accused Turkey's musicians, artists and authors of collaborating with terrorists.

'Politicians still do such things, but when you look at society in general, lots has changed and many things are accomplished. People can talk freely about their sense of injustice and about unjust things that were done to them. But those who organised military coups and massacres in Turkey's history also accomplished their own triumphs. All the aggrieved groups seem to be reduced to their own sufferings after all. We are forced to ignore the pains of others. Everyone therefore feels alone with their own grief. And this, I believe, has to change.'

Hours later the snow finally left Istanbul. I remembered Karakaşlı's words as I walked through the crowds gathering in Taksim Square on the anniversary of Hrant Dink's assassination. 'The rhetoric of democratisation is not at all convincing unless the Dink murder is conclusively solved,' she had said. 'I am not saying this as a close friend of Dink, and even less so as an Armenian. An injustice was done to a man who demanded justice, and until we pass the threshold that is the solving of his case, Turkey can hardly be called a democratic state.' The recent verdict in the murder trial outraged almost everyone in the country. The president, the prime minister, the leaders of the opposition, even the lawyers of the accused and the judge himself criticised the verdict for failing to acknowledge the political motives behind the murder. From the tragedy of Turkey's left to the tragedy of Turkey's dissidents, a sinister atmosphere hung over Taksim Square. As tourists looked in awe at the gradually growing crowd walking in the direction of *Agos*, I remembered Murat Belge's response when he saw how tens of thousands of people reacted to the murder committed five years ago.

At 3 o'clock sharp, the exact hour of Dink's assassination, Karakaşlı herself appeared on the balcony of the newspaper, saluting more than 40,000 people. Never have I seen so many marching together, even at the rallies of mainstream parties. This is the solidarity of those who have felt wronged by history, the solidarity of outsiders. 'Hrant is not a case to be closed,' Karakaşlı says in the same intimate voice she used with me a day earlier. 'No, he is not a court case. Hrant is an unclosed wound.' As the crowds took in the significance of these words, a sense of unity spread across their faces. For the first time that week I suddenly felt a little bit warmer. ❐

©Kaya Genç
41(1): 129/139
DOI: 10.1177/0306422012439022
www.indexoncensorship.org

Kaya Genç's first novel, *L'Avventura*, was published in 2009. He is a PhD candidate at the English literature department of Istanbul University and writes for Turkish and English publications

BREAKING THE SILENCE

Emin Milli

When I think about freedom of expression, I inevitably think about prison life in Azerbaijan. Prison is a very quiet place, unless the silence is disturbed by the screams of tortured prisoners or voices of guards demanding bribes. It is a place with its own traditions – icons, metaphors, heroes, rituals, narratives, unwritten laws – demanding unconditional obedience and silence. Demanding your legal rights, expressing your opinion openly or showing human solidarity with other inmates calling for justice usually results in severe punishment. Formal complaints are not encouraged and neither is expressing your views about how prison rules are applied. Prisoners often sew their mouths shut to make a statement or when demanding to see a lawyer. What a powerful symbol of an absurd reality: you have to sew your mouth shut to exercise the right to be heard by the system. In one of the most extreme cases in the jail I was in, one prisoner nailed his testicles to a bench to protest against the endless violation of his rights. I remember one veteran prisoner trying to explain to me the 'golden' survival rules of life in prison. The three magic words that protect your life and provide for your physical security are: *lal* (dumb), *kar* (deaf), *kor* (blind). He repeated it almost every day to me: 'You must stay *lal, kar, kor.*'

But this demand to stay *lal, kar and kor* is not limited to prisons. Azerbaijani society is reduced to the status of a passive observer in an imposed and enforced reality. You must observe the 'golden' rules of prison life in order to survive and to be able to protect yourself and those close to you. Under an authoritarian system, you are expected to practise a different form of freedom – the freedom of silence. It is you who chooses this freedom by coming to the 'right' conclusion. There is no need to impose repressions on a massive scale. Modern authoritarianism can afford to be smartly 'softist' and selective in its application of limitless, subtle or less subtle repressive measures.

Azerbaijan is no longer a society where you can promote or improve legislation or government practice in any meaningful way. Stealing public resources and holding rigged elections that present a veneer of legitimacy – whilst inviting the Council of Europe and other European institutions to observe and participate in this theatrical legitimisation of authoritarianism – discredit an already defunct discourse of freedom and democracy. Another memory overwhelms me: in 2010, prisoners were given ballots and instructed to put them into a ballot box in the presence of guards and the prison administrator. They were not allowed to look at the ballot papers to see whose name was ticked.

So, in such a system, what needs to be changed to support freedom of expression? The short answer is that the system itself needs to be completely changed. And one practical step would be to create an independent television station. Under the present circumstances this is only possible from abroad. A new generation of brave, well-educated and courageous Azerbaijanis must set up a channel outside the country and transmit its programming to Azerbaijan via satellite and the internet. It is extremely important to break the freedom of silence, to stop the fears that grip people's imaginations and to create platforms for social mobilisation both inside and outside the country. Time invested in non-existent dialogue, imaginary engagement, improving this or that bit of legislation, hope for reform is all wasted time. These efforts only help to prolong the status quo. Any contract between the government and its citizens and any opportunities for reform, if they ever existed, are now broken. The latest media tools and technologies must be used to disrupt the system, to break the silence. Some Arab nations have done it, Russians are doing it, and Azerbaijan can too. The new generation must bring about a democratic brotherhood with unbending courage that will prevail in our Land of Fire. ❐

©Emin Milli
41(1): 140/141
DOI: 10.1177/0306422012438988
www.indexoncensorship.org

Emin Milli is a writer and journalist. After criticising the government in 2009, he spent 16 months in prison

Don Mattera
Open letter to South African whites

Don Mattera is a black South African poet and a journalist with the Johannesburg Star. In November 1973 he was served with a Government Banning Order, which was renewed in November 1978. This means he will remain banned until 31 October 1983.

Last September, Don Mattera wrote an 'Open Letter to the White People of South Africa', an edited version of which appears below. Poems by Don Mattera were published in Index on Censorship 2/1975 *and an excerpt from his ' Autobiography' in* Index 5/1978.

To you, I may be just another name. Just another number in a sea of black faces. To your government and to your Secret Police, I am a PERSONA NON GRATA ... An enemy of the State who must be silenced or destroyed.

To those true Black people, who share with me a destiny as Children of Africa, I firmly believe that I am a spokesman for Justice and Freedom and Equality ... A man moved by the plight and pain of my oppressed brothers and sisters.

I am addressing you as a nation and at the same time, I am also aware that many valiant white men and women have raised their voices, offered their lives and the lives of their families in the cause of freedom for all people. I am constantly mindful of their great sacrifice and I know and am convinced that they will forever be enshrined in the hearts of Black people.

I have chosen an Open Letter, because your government has arbitrarily denied me my right publicly to express my feelings. My writings have been outlawed and nothing that I say can be published. My very thoughts are branded a danger to the security of the State, which in the final analysis, is REALLY YOU.

Since the crimes you and your government have perpetrated against my people are innumerable and since I lack the courage to rise up against you in their name, and most of all because I hate

Don Mattera

violence; I will confine this letter to the irreparable damage you and your government have personally caused me and my family.

Until this day, I have ever been united with those who suffer, are poor; with the sick and the dying. It was an inheritance from my family.

Yet for nearly six years now, with four more to follow, perhaps until I die, your government has summarily cut me, and countless others, off from that very vital and precious life-giving force called HUMAN INTERACTION.

Perhaps your government has told YOU why it took the criminal decision to deny and rob me and my colleagues of all social, political and human intercourse with our fellow beings, making

PERSONA NON GRATA

Banned writer **Don Mattera** wrote an 'open letter to the white people of South Africa' expressing the depths of his frustration

To you, I may be just another name. Just another number in a sea of black faces. To your government and to your Secret Police, I am a PERSONA NON GRATA … An enemy of the State who must be silenced or destroyed. To those true Black people, who share with me a destiny as Children of Africa, I firmly believe that I am a spokesman for Justice and Freedom and Equality … A man moved by the plight and pain of my oppressed brothers and sisters.

I am addressing you as a nation and at the same time I am also aware that many valiant white men and women have raised their voices, offered their lives and the lives of their families in the cause of freedom for all people. I am constantly mindful of their great sacrifice and I know and am convinced that they will forever be enshrined in the hearts of Black people.

I have chosen an Open Letter, because your government has arbitrarily denied me my right publicly to express my feelings. My writings have been outlawed and nothing that I say can be published. My very thoughts are branded a danger to the security of the State which, in the final analysis, is REALLY YOU. Since the crimes you and your government perpetrated against my people are innumerable and since I lack the courage to rise up against you in their name, and most of all because I hate violence, I will confine this letter to the irreparable damage you and your government have personally caused me and my family.

Until this day, I have ever been united with those who suffer, are poor; with the sick and the dying. It was an inheritance from my family. Yet for nearly six years now, with four more to follow, perhaps until I die, your government has summarily cut me, and countless others, off from that very vital and precious life-giving force called HUMAN INTERACTION.

Perhaps your government has told YOU why it took the criminal decision to deny and rob me and my colleagues of all social, political and human intercourse with our fellow-beings, making it a crime even to speak to a group of children. I was given no reason whatsoever.

And did any of you ask your government why I am prohibited from attending my daughter's birthday party? Or why I must wait outside a hall when my own son is being handed a trophy or a badge? Or why I have to ask your Chief Magistrate for permission to attend the funeral of a loved one or a friend or a great leader? Have any of you ever been prohibited from weeping at a graveside? Well, I have been.

Have any of you white people experienced the horror of raids by the Secret Police? Do you know how humiliating it is to hear that loud and vicious banging at the door, and watch helplessly as armed police search the house, pulling blankets off the sleeping children? Searching, scratching and stamping, until the whole damn house is filled with hatred and anger.

Have any Afrikaner mothers or wives ever sat up wide-eyed on their beds, afraid and bewildered with tears flowing uncontrollably as the husband is bundled into a police vehicle? Well, my wife has. And, has any white ten-year-old boy ever run barefoot into the night to the waiting police car and, with his fragile fists, banged against the door, crying and screaming as his father is taken away to some cold and dark cell, perhaps never to return again? My little son has done just that. And it is the same child that rushes to switch off the television set when your South African flag and your anthem appear at the end of the programmes.

I am not telling you these things out of self-pity. Nor do I want to be unbanned. These things are being said so that you, unlike the German nation, cannot tomorrow say: 'BUT WE DID NOT KNOW...' For you there must be no excuse.

History will be the judge.

I don't think that you can answer these questions unless you are a HELEN JOSEPH, a BRAAM FISCHER or a BEYERS NAUDE. Or any of those white men and women who have stood up to be counted, and are dead or suffering as a result of their consciences. Also, I don't think you have the capacity for such remorse as would move me to say: 'Forgive them for they know not what they do...' You know what you do. And what is being done in your name.

Yes, day by day, bitterness and anger overwhelm me, robbing me of clear thoughts, transforming me to a near vegetable. I have been so demeaned that I can no longer truly fulfill myself as a poet or a person. And today, my children, affected by this terrible change in me, reflect the bitterness I carry within my heart. I don't know why, though I have tried very hard, I cannot hate you. But my children watch me closely: laughing when I laugh, crying when I am sad. Asking me, forever asking me why it is that I endure so much pain and humiliation. Or why the setting sun no longer moves me. Or why I have rejected Christianity.

They will find the answers.

And no doubt this letter will hurt and offend you and your government, especially your Secret Police. If I know you, as I know your rulers, these words will spur you to vengeance and violence against me. Against my family. It has happened before, but I do not care. I am prepared to die. ❑

©Don Mattera
41(1): 142/145
DOI: 10.1177/0306422012438317
www.indexoncensorship.org

From the Archive 1980

Don Mattera is a South African poet and journalist. He was served with a Government Banning Order in 1973 which was renewed in 1978. At the time of writing, he faced another three years of being banned. This is an edited extract of his open letter. It first appeared in *Index on Censorship* Volume 9, Number 1, February 1980.

MANIFESTO

ALL CHANGE

Buya Jammeh

Under Gambian President Yahya Jammeh's 17-year rule, there have been widespread violations of human rights and basic freedoms. Journalists work in an environment of persistent threats, arbitrary arrests and torture and are frequently handed down prison terms on charges of sedition.

Last year was no exception. Nanama Keita, former deputy editor-in-chief and sports editor at the *Daily Observer*, and Dodou Sanneh were both charged with giving false information to a public officer; Keita fled the country in September. His colleague Saikou Ceesay was arrested in November after he paid a surety for Keita. In August, the National Intelligence Agency took out an injunction against independent community radio station Teranga FM, prohibiting it from broadcasting in the local language. After the civil resistance group Coalition for Change in The Gambia (CCG) was set up, many people were punished for their association with the movement, including one-time information minister Dr Amadou Scatred Janneh, former president of the Gambia Press Union, Ndey Tapha Sosseh, Mathew K Jallow and Famara Demba, who were all charged with sedition and treason.

On 24 November, Jammeh was re-elected for a fourth term. As press freedom advocates predicted, the election fell short of international standards and journalists and observers were intimidated and harassed. A few weeks later, on 16 December 2011, the country marked the seven-year anniversary of Deyda Hydara's murder. Hydara, who was gunned down in a Banjul suburb, was founder and co-proprietor of independent newspaper the *Point*. His murderers remain at large and, after several years without any serious investigation into the case, two of his children, supported by international NGOs, filed a suit at the Economic Community of West African States (Ecowas) community court, demanding that the authorities conduct a full investigation.

Daily Observer reporter Chief Ebrima Manneh disappeared in 2006. Evidence suggests that he was picked up by National Intelligence Agency officials, but the government vehemently rejects this. Justice Minister Edu Gomez told local media that Manneh was alive but that he was not in the government's custody as it is alleged. In an interview in September, Gambian Vice President Isatou Njie-Saidy stated that Manneh hadn't been arrested. 'There are people who die in the desert; anything can happen to anybody', she said, dashing the hopes of both Manneh's family and the journalism community. Both unresolved cases continue to have a significant effect on Gambian journalists and their work.

Yet Jammeh, a military-turned-civilian ruler, claims the Gambia enjoys freedom of the press and expression and points to a recent example of more than ten privately-run radio stations being issued with licences. He accuses many who work in the independent press of being mouthpieces for opposition parties, though he provides no proof for this and has made no comment about the behaviour of the staff of the Gambia Radio and Television Services (GRTS), who openly demonstrate their allegiance to the ruling party. In an interview with the privately-owned *Daily News*, Justice Minister Gomez dismissed suggestions of human rights abuses in the country as 'mere speculation'. In the same interview, Gomez threatened to prosecute any exiled Gambian who dared criticise the government's actions.

The country is in need of proper training for journalists and a media regulatory body. In spite of the challenges it faces, the Gambia Press Union supports practising journalists and has introduced journalism training and courses on international freedom of expression standards, supported by European partners and donors. Recently, the African Commission on Human and Peoples' Rights granted the Gambia Press Union observer status.

But the government must take positive steps towards supporting free expression in the country. It must stop arbitrary arrests, detention and intimidation of journalists; repeal the laws on sedition, libel and false publication; enact a freedom of information act; conduct independent and effective investigations into all cases of ill-treatment, torture and extra-judicial treatment of journalists, media professionals and human rights defenders and, crucially, order independent investigations into the Hydara and Manneh cases. ❐

©Buya Jammeh
41(1): 146/147
DOI: 10.1177/0306422012439371
www.indexoncensorship.org

Buya Jammeh is a journalist, human rights advocate and producer of the radio project Voice for Gambians

CONTENTS

Volume 23 (New Series) No 3 July/August 1994

STANDING IN THE QUEUE

Nadine Gordimer witnessed the end of apartheid in South Africa when the black population voted for the first time on an historic day

Is there any South African for whom this day will be remembered by any event – even the most personal – above its glowing significance as the day on which we voted? Even for whites, all of whom have had the vote since they were 18, this was the first time. This was my overwhelming sense of the day: the other elections, with their farcical show of a democratic procedure restricted to whites (and, later, to everyone but the black majority), had no meaning for any of us as South Africans: only as a hegemony of the skin.

Standing in the queue this morning, I was aware of a sense of silent bonding. Businessmen in their jogging outfits, nurses in uniform (two, near me, still wearing the plastic mob-caps that cover their hair in the cloistered asepsis of the operating theatre), women in their Zionist Church outfits, white women and black women who shared the mothering of white and black children winding about their legs, people who had brought folding stools to support their patient old bones, night watchmen just off duty, girl students tossing long hair the way horses switch their tails – here we all were as we have never been.

We have stood in line in banks and post offices together, yes, since the desegregation of public places; but until this day there was always the unseen difference between us, far more decisive than the different colours of our skins: some of us had the right that is the basis of all rights, the symbolic X, the sign of a touch on the controls of polity, the mark of citizenship, and others did not. But today we stood on new ground. The abstract term 'equality' took on materiality as we moved towards the church hall polling station and the simple act, the drawing of an X, that ended over three centuries of privilege for some, deprivation of human dignity for others.

The first signature of the illiterate is the X. Before that there was only the thumb-print, the skin-impression of the powerless. I realised this with something like awe when, assigned by my local branch of the African National Congress to monitor procedures at a polling booth, I encountered black people who could not read or write. A member of the Independent Electoral Commission would guide them through what took on the solemnity of a ritual: tattered identity document presented, hands outstretched under the ultra violet light, hands sprayed with invisible ink, and meticulously folded ballot paper – a missive ready to be despatched for the future – placed in those hands. Then an uncertain few steps towards a booth, accompanied by the IEC person and one of the party agents to make sure that when the voter said which party he or she wished to vote for the X would be placed in the appropriate square. Several times I was that party agent and witnessed a man or woman giving this signature to citizenship. A strange moment: the first time man scratched the mark of his identity, the conscious proof of his existence, on a stone must have been rather like this.

Of course nearby in city streets there were still destitute black children sniffing glue as the only substitute for nourishment and care; there were homeless families existing in rigged-up shelters in the crannies of the city. The law places the gown of equality underfoot; it did not feed the hungry or put up a roof over the head of the homeless today, but it changed the base on which South African society was for so long built. The poor are still there, round the corner. But they are not The Outcast. They can no longer be decreed to be forcibly removed, deprived of land, and of the opportunity to change their lives. They count. The meaning of the counting of the vote, whoever wins the majority, is this, and not just the calculation of the contents of ballot boxes.

If to be alive on this day was not Wordsworth's 'very heaven' for those who have been crushed to the level of wretchedness by the decades of apartheid and the other structures of racism that preceded it, if they could not experience the euphoria I shared, standing in line, to be living at this hour has been extraordinary. The day has been captured for me by the men and women who couldn't read or write, but underwrote it, at last, with their kind of signature. May it be the seal on the end of illiteracy, of the pain of imposed ignorance, of the deprivation of the fullness of life. ❑

©Nadine Gordimer
41(1): 148/150
DOI: 10.1177/0306422012438316
www.indexoncensorship.org

Nadine Gordimer's many novels include *No Time Like the Present* (Bloomsbury) and *Burger's Daughter* (Jonathan Cape). She was awarded the Nobel Prize in Literature in 1991. This essay first appeared in *Index on Censorship*, July/August 1994, Volume 23

SAQI BOOKS

UNDERSTANDING THE MIDDLE EAST IN REVOLT

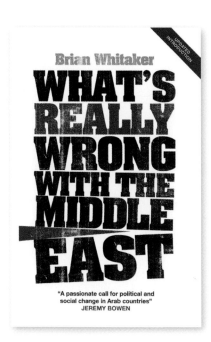

What's Really Wrong with the Middle East
Brian Whitaker

'A passionate call for political and social change in Arab countries' JEREMY BOWEN

'[Should] be required reading by Arab elites from the Atlantic to the Gulf' PATRICK SEALE

£10.99 978-1-84659-624-0

Unspeakable Love
Brian Whitaker

'Anyone interested in reform in the Arab world must read this book' MAI YAMANI

'Masterful – incredibly balanced and thoughtful'
BEN SUMMERSKILL

£10.99 978-1-84659-483-3

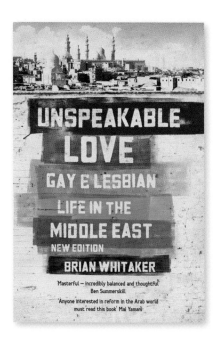

www.saqibooks.com

FREEDOM DENIED

Nic Dawes

To the surprise and disappointment of many South Africans who see the country's 15-year-old constitution as the enabling framework for democratic development in a complex and deeply fractured society, its most basic principles are coming under sustained attack, not from apartheid die-hards, but from the ANC itself.

Nowhere is this more immediately evident than in legislative proposals to limit freedom of the press, and of information more broadly, that are currently working their way through parliament thanks to the efforts of the security sector and of a ruling party that is increasingly hostile to South Africa's robustly free press.

In the coming months, the second chamber of the legislature, the National Council of Provinces, will be considering the Protection of State Information Bill, which has already been processed and approved by the National Assembly.

The law ostensibly aims to reform our apartheid-era classification regime, an important and necessary project. Unfortunately, it seems the spooks at the Ministry of State Security felt they couldn't miss an opportunity to tighten their control over sensitive information.

In its current form, and despite numerous improvements produced by nearly three years of lobbying and protest by journalists and civil society, the bill is a clear and present danger to the free flow of information that our constitution envisages as central to the architecture of democracy.

It makes possession or disclosure of classified information – no matter by whom or for what reason – punishable by jail terms of up to 25 years. Activists, journalists and others who reveal government secrets in an effort to show serious wrongdoing by the state will not be able to argue in defence that they did so in the public interest.

This isn't just a concern for reporters worried about the conduct of the army and intelligence services (the bill gives them extraordinary and unwarranted protection from scrutiny). On the contrary, some of the most cogent opposition has come from poor communities, worried that corruption is robbing them of access to clean water, adequate housing and electricity. Because any organ of state can opt into the classification system, they worry that security concerns will be trumped up as an excuse to keep evidence of graft and mismanagement out of the public domain.

If no major changes are made during this final leg of the parliamentary process, the bill's opponents will ask the constitutional court to throw it out on the grounds that it is inimical to our bill of rights.

Even as that process unfolds, a potentially more serious threat is taking shape. Despite Nelson Mandela's recognition of the centrality of free press to democracy, many in the ANC feel that South Africa's print media, which has been vigorous in investigating official corruption, incompetence and hypocrisy, needs reigning in.

They are gearing up to begin a parliamentary process aimed at introducing statutory print media regulation that would extend political control over newspapers that have remained stubbornly immune to interference.

In broad outline, the party proposes to create a 'Media Appeals Tribunal' that is styled as providing ethical oversight of print media and redress for those aggrieved by their treatment in the press. Members of this body would be appointed by parliament and given the power to levy fines and impose other, as yet undetermined, sanctions.

There is broad recognition among South African journalists of the importance of ethical rigour and of methods to secure quick and inexpensive redress when ethical boundaries are transgressed. There are already overlapping institutions of press accountability and a very active discussion about how to improve them. What we cannot accept is a statutory regime that would lead to the licensing of newspapers and journalists and give political commissars the whip-hand over our coverage.

The South African debate matters not just for our new and complicated country, but for a continent that is struggling to emerge from decades of press controls, first under colonial administration and then under post-liberation governments. We want to continue to lead the wave of openness that is sweeping across the continent, not to serve as an object lesson in how awkward voices can be silenced. A broad and vigorous coalition against these proposals is building in South Africa, but international solidarity will be critical if we are to win the battle. ❑

©Nic Dawes
41(1): 152/153
DOI: 10.1177/0306422012439646
www.indexoncensorship.org

Nic Dawes is editor-in-chief of the *Mail and Guardian*

Ⴕⴚⴄ Ⴒⴄⴊⴄⴂⴐⴀⴔⴑ
Ways With Words
Festival of Words and Ideas

Dartington Hall
Devon
6 – 15 July 2012

Ten days of books, ideas and inspiration in the heart of the South Devon countryside.

Join world-class authors and speakers this summer as we celebrate the 21st Ways With Words festival; one of the UK's most loved literary events.

Set in the stunning medieval courtyard and gardens of Dartington Hall.

Full programme available in early May.

Call **01803 86 73 73**
or check online at
www.wayswithwords.co.uk

2012 programme to include

Michael Palin
Hilary Mantel
Claire Tomalin
Jeremy Vine
Joanne Harris
Andrew Miller
Mark Easton
Simon Jenkins
Michael Buerk
Roy Hattersley
Michael Frayn

... and many more

THELONGVIEW

Judith Vidal-Hall remembers the day censorship was pronounced dead and buried

In 1992, *Index* received a letter from one of its major funders in the US. It thanked us for our invaluable work in bringing the Cold War to a satisfactory conclusion and recommended we use the remaining funds in the kitty to wind up in an orderly manner: 'Thank you for everything you have done over the years. Go home. There is no more censorship.'

The perception that *Index* was associated with the Cold War politics of the US stems, no doubt, from the relationship of Stephen Spender, one of *Index*'s founding fathers, with the CIA-funded magazine *Encounter*. Though he resigned as editor as soon as the source of funding was made explicit, the rumours surrounding *Index* persisted, even though it is apparent from the earliest issues that this was by no means the case.

In its first year, the magazine included searching articles on the military dictatorships then dominant in southern Europe, notably Greece, the repression of free expression by the quasi-dictatorship in Argentina and other Latin American states, and a monitor – 'Index Index', still an essential part of the magazine – which recorded infringements of free expression across the world. Censorship, evidently, was not confined to the eastern bloc.

The magazine was re-launched in May 1994 with a seminal piece by Ronald Dworkin, 'New Map of Censorship', that set the agenda for the coming years and, incidentally, scotched once and for all any lingering doubt as to *Index*'s political associations. As Dworkin implied in his essay, censorship is part of the human condition, wherever those in power reduce the marginalised and excluded to silence. And power resides not only with governments: racism, xenophobia, prejudice – against the Roma in much of Europe, for instance – effectively deny people a voice and a presence in society. Censorship does not end, it merely changes its guise and shifts location. As Dworkin wrote:

End of an era, but not the end of censorship. Tearing down the Berlin Wall, 1989
Credit: Sipa Press/Rex Features

Index was founded in the conviction that freedom of speech, along with the allied freedoms of conscience and religion, are fundamental human rights ... But that strong conviction is suddenly challenged not only by freedom's oldest enemies – the despots and ruling thieves who fear it – but also by new enemies who claim to speak for justice not tyranny, and who point to other values we respect, including self-determination, equality and freedom from racial hatred and prejudice, as reasons why the right of free speech should now be demoted to a much lower grade of urgency and importance.

As the century turned, we not only saw conflict on a wider scale, we watched silence fall in parts of the world we had always thought immune to censorship. In the wake of 9/11, it was not only the United States that imposed silence through such legislation as the Patriot Act. As the 'war on terror' got into its stride, it was used by countries as far away as Russia, many newly independent countries in Eastern Europe and even within the more established democracies to silence criticism and dissent. Political correctness, another US invention, the fear of imposing western values on multicultural societies, such as the UK, and the 'hate speech' that came to characterise religious debate imposed further restrictions on free expression. However worthy the motives behind such attitudes, the effect was all too familiar: the censorship of protest and unwelcome opinion. As Dworkin concluded:

When we compromise on freedom because we think our immediate goals more important, we are likely to find that the power to exploit the compromise is not in our hands after all, but in those of fanatical priests armed with *fatwas* and fanatical moralists with their own brand of hate.

It is this that *Index* uniquely continues to expose and criticise with the energy and conviction that marked its first issue 40 years ago. Not only in places such as China, 'freedom's oldest enemy', but closer to home among those 'who claim to speak for justice not tyranny'. ❐

©Judith Vidal-Hall
41(1): 155/158
DOI: 10.1177/0306422012438684
www.indexoncensorship.org

Judith Vidal-Hall was editor of *Index on Censorship* from 1993 until 2006

REX

Rex Features
Serving the world's media

We support free speech

BIRD ON A WING

Sidiqullah Tauhidi

After years of the tyrannic regime of the Taliban, the establishment of an interim government led to a new era for freedom of speech in Afghanistan. An international community keen to create opportunities, coupled with media law reform brought in by King Zahir Shah, paved the way for free media to flourish.

After Sardar Mohammad Daud Khan's coup, the fall of Babrak Karmal, the rule of the Mujahideen and the subsequent civil war, freedom of speech had been largely forgotten: only a small number of publications existed and most could not continue due to security concerns. During Taliban rule not a single independent media outlet functioned in the country.

In the last ten years, numerous media outlets have started in Afghanistan. According to local figures, there are currently 47 television stations, 147 radio stations, 24 newspapers, 71 weekly newspapers, 25 magazines and ten news agencies. Exercising one's right to free expression has become almost commonplace, at least in large cities. Free speech is now enshrined in the country's media law which, after many amendments, was passed on 5 July 2009. The Ministry of Culture and Information was tasked with developing a legal mechanism to safeguard press freedoms. Freedom of speech for citizens has also been guaranteed in the constitution.

Despite such progress, there remain significant obstacles, including security concerns. In the last ten years, 30 national and international reporters have been killed by local Taliban warlords and other unidentified assailants. Travelling can be dangerous and there is no protection for journalists. At times, government officials attempt to block print and broadcast media. According to local sources, there were 80 cases of violence against journalists in 2011, a 38 per cent increase since 2010. There are no efforts to bring those responsible to account, so that the journalism community works in a state of anxiety. There are also no legal safeguards against the arbitrary arrest of journalists.

As a result, many who may have considered a career in journalism pursue other employment. A low literacy rate, the absence of a newspaper-reading culture and self-censorship all take their toll. There are significant financial difficulties: many newspapers have closed down because they failed to attract advertising revenue, which largely goes to television and electronic media.

Initiatives to support free media in Afghanistan can be compared to a bird with only one wing. The government has failed to bring in much-needed reforms, despite demands from free speech advocates. Many laws are repressive and access to information rights do not exist. Some see free expression as a potential source of instability and a threat to security. In some cases, authorities place strict limitations on the media, waiting for the international community to shift its focus away from Afghanistan before introducing a more thorough form of censorship.

When the media reports on dangerous situations for journalists or, on the rare occasion that those responsible for violence are named, the government either fails to take action or even applies pressure to the media outlet concerned. This has seriously damaged the current political process and the country's move towards democracy. There is no choice but to strengthen civic freedoms and make them an important and valuable component of our democracy. We must demand commitment from the government – and the international community – to continue development in this area.

After ten years, the time has come to evaluate the situation in Afghanistan. Writers, poets, political activists, intellectuals, local media and the international community must make free speech the accepted norm. We must prevent the government from negotiating with its enemies, particularly with regard to free expression. ❑

©Sidiqullah Tauhidi
41(1): 160/161
DOI: 10.11770306422012439377
www.indexoncensorship.org

Sidiqullah Tauhidi is a journalist and broadcaster

Eduardo Galeano
Voices of hope

Bad news for the engineers of horror: the death machine produces life. Every part is perfect, shining and in place, the cogs have been oiled and checked, the instructions from the most experienced and reputed international experts have been carried out to the letter. And yet, more alive than ever, there is the human soul, quivering. Isolated, tortured men, at grips with the daily treatment of destruction, retort by creating. A person who can write the following has not been broken, nor had his heartbeat stifled:

> Sometimes it rains
> and I love you
> sometimes the sun appears
> and I love you
> prison is sometimes
> always I love you.

These poems are anonymous. Their authors are prisoners in the Penal de Libertad (Freedom Prison, as a betrayal of language would have it), the main prison for political offenders in Uruguay. They were written on cigarette papers and have found their way out through the bars and thick walls of the concentration camp. Since they are the work of prisoners, they perfectly portray the situation of a country which itself is one huge prison:

> A fellow inmate said
> if we put aside
> orders
> regulations
> if we overlook
> uniforms
> bars
> if we don't count
> officers
> and their stool-pigeons
> a fellow inmate said
> and I believe him
> here
> in this great prison
> we are prisoners.

No. 5
Si VIERAS
LAS CONTRADICCIONES QUE HAY
EN EL EJÉRCITO
SI HUBIERAS ESCUCHADO
COMO DISCUTÍAN
ALFERES, CAPITAN
MIENTRAS ME DABAN

No. 6
A VECES LLUEVE
Y TE QUIERO
A VECES SALE EL SOL
Y TE QUIERO
LA CARCEL ES A VECES
SIEMPRE TE QUIERO

No. 7
¿ME OÍS?
YO DIJE Q. TE CONOCÍ EN UN BAILE
QUE NOS PRESENTO PEDRO
¿ME OÍS?
YO DIJE Q. FUE DIEGO

Poem written on cigarette paper in a Uruguayan jail

The prison is everyone's home. Is there anyone who hasn't had the right to speak abolished? A recent order by the Uruguayan dictatorship's National Public Relations Board forbids anyone under the rank of general in the armed forces from expressing a political opinion. All the country's inhabitants are hostages on parole, with no rights beyond breathing and obeying. Simply to collect a trade union subscription is seen as an incitement to crime and is punishable by six years' imprisonment. At the point where, in the score of the national anthem, the chorus should shout out 'Tyrants, tremble!', the music has now been made soft so that the singers are forced to whisper the phrase. Anyone who did dare to sing out loudly would be heading straight for the electric torture prod and jail. Between 1968 and 1975, when there was still an opposition press, the regime beat the world record for suspensions and

VOICES OF HOPE

Eduardo Galeano found the human spirit undiminished in the poems of Uruguayan political prisoners, smuggled out of jail more than 30 years ago

Bad news for the engineers of horror: the death machine produces life. Every part is perfect, shining and in place, the cogs have been oiled and checked, the instructions from the most experienced and reputed international experts have been carried out to the letter. And yet, more alive than ever, there is the human soul, quivering. Isolated, tortured men, at grips with the daily treatment of destruction, retort by creating. A person who can write the following has not been broken, nor had his heartbeat stifled:

> Sometimes it rains
> and I love you
> sometimes the sun appears
> and I love you
> prison is sometimes
> always I love you.

These poems are anonymous. Their authors are prisoners in the Penal de Libertad (Freedom Prison, as a betrayal of language would have it), the main prison for political offenders in Uruguay. They were written on cigarette papers and have found their way out through the bars and thick walls of the concentration camp. Since they are the work of prisoners, they perfectly portray the situation of a country which itself is one huge prison:

> A fellow inmate said
> if we put aside
> orders
> regulations

if we overlook
uniforms
bars
if we don't count
officers
and their stool-pigeons
a fellow inmate said
and I believe him
here
in this great prison
we are prisoners.

The prison is everyone's home. Is there anyone who hasn't had the right to speak abolished? A recent order by the Uruguayan dictatorship's National Public Relations Board forbids anyone under the rank of general in the armed forces from expressing a political opinion. All the country's inhabitants are hostages on parole, with no rights beyond breathing and obeying. Simply to collect a trade union subscription is seen as an incitement to crime and is punishable by six years' imprisonment. At the point where, in the score of the national anthem, the chorus should shout out 'Tyrants, tremble!', the music has now been made soft so that the singers are forced to whisper the phrase. Anyone who did dare to sing out loudly would be heading straight for the electric torture prod and jail.

Anyone who dared to sing would be heading straight for torture

Uruguay has proportionately the largest budget for repression in the world. This profligacy by the military and police could perhaps be explained by the fact that the government, according to a recent armed forces document published by the national university, considers that we are in the midst of the third world war against international subversion. In fact, the military in my country are waging a very different kind of war. For the Uruguayan armed forces, who now act as the political party representing the multinational corporations, the enemy is the people itself:

Green
but mutters
green
but talks
green
but interrogates
green
but tortures.

Uruguayan political prisoners can only speak by telephone to the rare visitors they are allowed, and they are forbidden to look round, wink, to walk either more quickly or more slowly than normal, and for some strange reason are forbidden to draw fish, pregnant women and worms. They also have to pay an average of $500 per annum for their lodging, as though the prison were a hotel. There are frequent attempts at suicide in the punishment cells, and equally frequent simulated firing squads. But these poems do not complain. They are not soiled with self-pity. They are written out of dignity rather than misery:

To have a quick word with the bee
in its buzzing flight
to tell the ant to hurry
with the bread
for his lady wife
to contemplate the spider
admire the beauty
of its amazing feet
and beg it
to climb more slowly up its web
all these are ways
of resisting.
Out of dignity, fought for and rescued each day:
Today they took off my hood
How can I cry now
just at this very moment
I so feel like crying?
Where would I hide my tears now?
Now they have taken off the hood.
Defeat for the inquisitors and the executioners.
Popular culture can't be contained by any prison,

Can't be kept out by any customs barrier, can't be
killed by any bullet:
Why on earth does the sergeant
whistle Viglietti
why on earth does the corporal
hum the Olimareños
why on earth does the private
sing Zitarrosa
how come they've so much
shit in their heads?

In classical Chinese opera, the emperor beheads any messenger who brings bad news. Our true national culture was bringing bad news for those in power when the military, knife clenched between the teeth, flung themselves into the attack against centres of learning, publishers, newspapers, theatres, art galleries, carnival dancing and popular celebrations. This was the highest tribute ever paid to Uruguayan culture, for what is one to think of a culture that could stay free in a society in chains? Censorship, prison, exile, were waiting for the guilty. The dictatorship punishes anyone who believes that the country should not be a prison or an old people's home. In the end, books are banned in just the same way as meetings.

These poems by political prisoners are the work of precisely this 'common man', who is not content to consume the sparse or non-existent permitted culture, but who is capable of creating it for himself. The people's creative energy never dies, although it may sometimes appear to be asleep; nor does it figure among the lists of possessions of those who own the country and the official culture, which praises death and pays homage to fear. In the darkness of his cell, man is searching for symbols of identity, signs of life. ❏

©Eduardo Galeano
41(1): 162/166
DOI: 10.1177/0306422012438314
www.indexoncensorship.org

Eduardo Galeano is a Uruguayan journalist and novelist. His works include *Memory of Fire* (Pantheon Books) and *Open Veins of Latin America* (Monthly Review Press). This is an edited version of an article first published in *Index on Censorship* Volume 9, Number 5, October 1980.

Making voices heard
since 1903

BAD LUCK

Cuban poets have to toe the official line if they want to get on. **Jorge Olivera Castillo** on the good fortune he'd prefer to do without

Cuba has both lucky and unlucky poets. The lucky ones can leave the country without having to confront the military bureaucrats of the Home Office [Ministry of Immigration and Overseas] that hands out permits.

Lucky poets have frequently devoted a great many years to being submissive and efficient functionaries within the hierarchies of the Ministry of Culture that, with few exceptions, employ long tried and tested instruments of coercion to maintain control of writers, artists and intellectuals.

The truth is that there are very few among the so-called lucky poets who can convince us of even a partial independence within a sector where rules have clearly defined features. One way or another, the lucky chancers become obliged to compromise and, at some point in time, to renounce every belief, opinion and even motive in order to get their respective works off the blacklist and onto the page.

The manner in which censorship is exercised remains concealed behind a type of reasoning so obscure it is scarcely comprehensible. This is in turn relayed to foreign observers of the Cuban cultural panorama, ever since the advent of the revolutionary period that would later become a dictatorship.

It is extremely hard to avoid submitting to such bureaucratic manoeuvres, whether one is seeking authorisation for a trip abroad, the official consent essential to have a book published, or the award of a national prize for literature. All literary prizes, in whatever form (whether as cash, a computer, a stipend, or even a car), come within the aegis of a structure headed up by high-ranking politicians and generals inside the Ministry of the Interior.

If a writer creates a difficult situation for the powers that be, they are relegated to publications with miniscule print-runs and a total dearth of advertising or any other form of publicity to promote the writer within national literature.

The 'luck' of the lucky poets who get to participate in international poetry events comes at a very high price. Speaking personally, I never received any such privilege when I was awarded a scholarship by Harvard University's Department of Literature, inviting me for the academic year 2010–2011 [Harvard University is currently looking to renew the invitation of an Honorary Chair to Jorge Olivera for the academic year 2012–2013].

The letter of invitation from the Centre of Studies never reached my hands. It has remained stalled – for nearly two years now – in either the Cuban Consulate in Washington, the International Legal Consultancy in Havana, or one of the offices of the Interior Ministry. Without the original signed version of the letter, it has proved impossible to obtain the necessary documents to leave the country.

The 'luck' of the poet-functionary is scarcely recognised evidence of his ambiguous loyalties. When forthcoming histories come to be written, these poets will appear like black holes in an intellectual sector that, with very few exceptions, opted for silence, double standards, or a pact with the rulers of this freak show that still bears the name of the Cuban Revolution. ❐

Edited and translated by Amanda Hopkinson
©Jorge Olivera Castillo
41(1): 168/169
DOI: 10.1177/0306422012439645
www.indexoncensorship.org

Jorge Olivera Castillo is a writer, poet and journalist. He was imprisoned in 2003 following a crackdown on dissidents and released the following year, on condition that he refrain from political journalism

By way of Introduction

Bringing the past to light: the Lubianka's hidden treasure

Interview with Vitaly Shentalinsky by Irena Maryniak

Vitaly Shentalinsky is a representative of the Commission for the Lost Literary Legacy of the Soviet Union, founded in Moscow in the mid-1980s. The Commission collects and arranges publication of material by writers persecuted or imprisoned by the Soviet authorities before *perestroika*. A major outlet is the popular magazine *Ogonyok,* where Shentalinsky regularly displays his more spectacular discoveries. In November 1990, he was invited to give a seminar at St Antony's College, Oxford. **Irena Maryniak** spoke to him there.

*

IM. How was the Commission launched and who initiated the idea?

VS. It began as a writers' pressure group. We knew that quantities of

literature were still locked in secret government archives. During house searches, arrests or raids on editorial offices, anything apparently seditious was confiscated. When a writer was arrested, his archive usually disappeared with him. We estimate that about 2,000 writers were imprisoned; that's a conservative figure. Around 1,500 died. Hundreds vanished. Nobody knows what became of them, or where they are buried. All documentation about them was falsified. Their manuscripts are the most important evidence we have.

There were doubts and misgivings about what we could do, of course. People maintained that everything had been burnt and warned that we would never be admitted into the Lubianka.

Irena Maryniak with Vitaly Shentali at *Index,* London, December 1990

IM. Did you have much support fr the Writers' Union?

VS. No. We began independently a group of writers who shared similar v Our more prominent members includ Bulat Okudzhava, Yury Karyakin, Vik Astafev, Vladimir Makanin . . . It took about two years before we gained acc the Lubianka archives. We met with resistance, of course: a kind of elastic which gave a little and then sent us rig back to where we had started. There a officials who have no interest in seeing material made public. Many were inve in the cases I examine; writers frequen informed on their colleagues. Some are still living, and very comfortably too.

THELONGVIEW

Andrew Graham-Yooll on a hit literary year that included Bulgakov and *Death and the Maiden*

When the Berlin Wall came down, Russia, the most powerful member of the federation that replaced the Soviet Union, became a field for fortune hunters and new millionaires. So why not authors' rights and royalties? Into the *Index* office one Spring morning marched Vitaly Shentalinsky of the Moscow Writers' Union. He unloaded a bag full of goodies on the desk of director and publisher Philip Spender: the writings had been held in the bowels of the Union, deposited there in an act of bureaucratic self-preservation by KGB agents who had seized them from their prisoners. We could only marvel at the names listed for we could not read Russian. Irena Maryniak, our Eastern Europe editor, was called in and after a glance expressed her delight – 'How can we have them?' she asked (read Irena Maryniak on Russia, pp.85-95). Shentalinsky wanted money; we did not have the funds. I asked if I could check the copy with Irena, most of it printed in editions of *Ogonyok* magazine. She sat by our unreliable photocopier. I prayed that this time it would not fail. I copied as fast as I could, threw the copies on Irena's desk and returned to Spender's office with the magazines.

The result was a jumbo edition for August/September 1991. The cover read 'USSR: the hidden literary treasure of the Lubianka'. It included the diary of Mikhail Bulgakov, the interrogation of Osip Mandelstam, an unknown novel by Andrei Platonov, Isaac Babel's case file and an interview with Vitaly Shentalinsky. He deserved the credit for gaining access to the archives. I felt very proud.

Shentalinsky had spent months campaigning for access to the Lubianka. When writers were arrested their archive usually disappeared with them. Shentalinsky estimated that at least 2,000 writers had been imprisoned. Hundreds vanished and around 1,500 died. Their manuscripts were the most important evidence that survived. The first success came in 1989 when access was granted to Isaac Babel's case file. 'As a society we are still shell-shocked from the Lubianka terror,' Shentalinsky told Irena Maryniak. 'Now they're inviting us to get up and dance, and people won't. It'll take two generations to resolve. If you give a slave his freedom he'll treat it as yet another arbitrary act. He'll snatch at what was repressed within himself and make slaves of those around him.'

We were savouring our success when the Chilean author Ariel Dorfman called to ask me if we would publish his new play *Scars on the Moon* (Luna que se quiebra). The title came from a romantic all-time favourite bolero by Mexican composer Agustín Lara. The play was a chilling account of a Chilean woman encountering the man who had tortured her during the Pinochet regime. I told Ariel Dorfman we had a budget of one hundred pounds and that was it. He said he had expected a bit more, but relented (read an extract from Ariel Dorfman's new play, pp. 181-199).

Dorfman had returned to live in Chile from the US the previous year. In an interview published alongside the play, he told me: 'Basically, there will always be a co-existence in many societies between those who committed crimes and those who were repressed. This co-existence is a fact of contemporary society. It does not happen only in the Chilean transition to democracy, which in its own way is very Chilean. It happens in all transitions – in Eastern Europe and elsewhere. We call the situation created *la impunidad* – the state of impunity. We have to understand what we have done to ourselves, and that somehow we can stop.

'The point about the play is that it works in the grey zone of ambiguity. It allows each person in the audience, or each reader, to ask themselves who they are in relation to each character. In Chile, everybody has lived that situation. How do you make the truth, how do you pervert one truth to bring out another?'

Within weeks, the title of the play had changed to *Death and the Maiden* and opened at the Royal Court Upstairs, thanks in many ways to Harold Pinter. In October 1991, Nick Hern published the Royal Court edition. Then came Roman Polanski's film. The play had outgrown us. That was as it should be. ❏

©Andrew Graham-Yooll
41(1): 170/172
DOI: 10.1177/0306422012438648
www.indexoncensorship.org

Andrew Graham-Yooll was editor of Index from 1989 to 1993. His latest essay in English is *Who Do You Think You Are?* in the Seagull manifesto series. His most recent book is a bilingual anthology of Argentine poets, published in Buenos Aires

UNDER THE IRON HEEL

Mikhail Bulgakov's diary was confiscated during a house search in 1929 – and published in English for the first time in *Index*

The extract from Bulgakov's diary below was reproduced from a typewritten copy made by the OGPU (forerunner of the KGB) and discovered in the Lubianka secret police headquarters. Bulgakov had demanded the return of his diaries when they were seized – and then promptly destroyed them. So it is, ironically, thanks to the Soviet secret police that the diaries of 1923-25 survive. As *Index* reported at the time: 'The diary offers a unique insight into Bulgakov's mind at a point in his career for which information is otherwise scarce.'

1923

2 September. Sunday.

Today I went with [the writer Valentin] Kataev to see Aleksey Tolstoy at his dacha in Ivankovo. He was very pleasant today. The only thing I don't like about him is the incorrigibly bohemian manner in which he and his wife treat young writers. Everything, however, is redeemed by his truly great talent. When Kataev and I were taking our leave, he accompanied us as far as the weir. A half moon in the sky, a starry evening, quietness. Tolstoy talked about the need to found a school. He even softened a little. 'Let's take an oath, looking at the moon.'

He is bold, but he seeks support in me and Kataev. His thoughts about literature are always accurate and apt, sometimes magnificently so. In the midst of my depression and yearning for the past, sometimes, as at the moment, in the absurdly cramped surroundings of this vile room in a vile house, I have surges of confidence in myself and my strength. Even now I can feel my thought soaring and I know that I am immeasurably more gifted as a writer than anyone else around me. But in conditions like the present I might just buckle at the knees.

3 September. Monday.

After a dreadful summer we are now having a glorious autumn. The past few days we've had sunshine and it's been warm. Every day I go to work in my Gudok (The Hooter), where I quite pointlessly kill time the whole day. There is not much money and I am living, as always, above my modest means. You eat and drink well, but there's nothing left for other things. Not a day passes without the accursed swill – beer. Today too I was in a beer parlour on Strastnaya Square with Aleksey Tolstoy, Kalmens, and of course the lame 'captain' who follows the Count [Tolstoy] like a shadow.

30 (17 Old Style) September.

[*At the end of the 16th century when most of Europe adopted the Gregorian or New Style calendar the Russians retained the Julian or Old Style calendar. The New Style calendar was formally adopted by the Soviet government in February 1918, by which time the difference between the two calendars had become 13 days.*]

Probably because I am a conservative to ... I wanted to write 'to the marrow of my bones', but that is cliched, so in a word, a conservative, on the old Church festivals I am drawn to my diary. What a pity I don't remember the precise date in September on which I arrived in Moscow two years ago. Two years. How much has changed in that time? A lot, of course. But all the same, the second anniversary of my arrival finds me still in the same room and still the same inside myself. I'm ill, to add to everything else.

First, about politics, always those same vile and unnatural politics. Germany is still in turmoil. The mark has begun to rise, however, because the Germans have stopped the passive resistance in the Ruhr, but there is a civil war going on in Bulgaria. There is fighting with the Communists. Wrangel's troops are defending the government. [*Wrangel was Commander-in-Chief of the White armies in the Russian Civil War from April 1920 and subsequently head of the 'emigre' movements.*] I have no doubt at all that these secondary Slav states, every bit as savage as Russia, offer splendid soil for the seeds of Communism. Our newspapers are exaggerating events every way they can, although, who knows, maybe the world is indeed splitting into two parts – Communism and Fascism. Nobody knows what's going to happen.

[...]

If I discard my imagined and real fears, I can admit that my life at present suffers from only one major defect: the lack of a flat. In literature I am making slow but definite progress. I know this for sure. The only problem is that I am never absolutely certain of the quality of what I have written. It is as if something films over my brain and cramps my hand when I have to describe ... what I know so deeply and genuinely in my thought and feeling.

22 October. Monday. Night.

[...]

Today at work in Gudok there was a real joke and no mistake. The 'Non-party Members' Initiative Group' proposed a meeting to discuss help for the German proletariat. When N opened the meeting the Communist R appeared, indignant and threatening, and declared that it was 'unheard of that non-party members should call their own meetings'. He demanded that the meeting be closed and a general meeting called. N went white and pointed out that the meeting had been – approved by the party cell. From then on it was simple. The non-party members voted as one that the party members should invite party members, and spoke flattering words. In response the party members appeared and put through a motion that they should give twice as much as non-party members – non-party members one day's pay, party members two days' pay – thereby spitting right in the face of the non-party nitwits.

[...]

26 October. Friday. Evening.

[...]

At moments of ill-health and loneliness I fall prey to sad and envious thoughts. I bitterly regret that I gave up medicine as a career and condemned myself to an uncertain existence. But God is my witness that I did it out of love for literature and for no other reason. Literature now is a hard profession. For me with my views ... it is hard to publish and make a living. My ill-health in these conditions is in the highest degree inopportune. But let's not lose heart. Today I looked through *The Last of the Mohicans*, which I bought recently for my library. What charm there is in that sentimental old Fennimore Cooper. David, who is always singing psalms, led me to the thought of God. Perhaps the strong and the bold do not need Him, but people like me find life easier with the thought of Him. My ill health has complications and is prolonged.

I am in very low spirits. Ill-health may prevent me from working and that is why I fear it, that is why I hope in God. As regards people, my presentiments never deceive me. Never. Some real scum is grouping round *Nakanune* (On the Eve). I can congratulate myself on being in their company. Oh, it's going to be very hard for me in the future when I have to scrape the dirt from my name. But I give honest account to myself of one thing: it was iron necessity that made me publish in *Nakanune*. If it had not been for *Nakanune* I could not have published *Zapiski na manzhetakh* (Notes on Shirt-Cuffs) nor many other pieces in which I was able to utter a truthful literary word. You have to be an exceptional hero to keep silent throughout four years, and keep silent without any hope that you will ever be able to open your mouth in the future. I, alas, am no hero. But now I have more courage. Oh, much more courage than in 1921. And were it not for my ill-health I would be looking with more confidence into my misty black future.

[...]

6 November (24 October). Tuesday. Evening.
Kolya G has just left. He is treating me for my illness. After he went I read Mikhail Chekhov's badly written, untalented book about his great brother. Am reading Gorky's masterly book *Moi universitety* [My Universities]. Now I am full of meditations and have begun to understand clearly: I have to stop laughing. Also: literature is now my whole life. I shall never return to medicine. I don't like Gorky as a person, but he is a hugely strong writer and what dreadful and important things he says about writing.

Today, at about five o'clock, I was at Lezhnev's. He told me two important things: first, that my story *Psalm* (in *Nakanune*) is a splendid miniature ('I would have published it'); second, that *Nakanune* is an object of general contempt and hatred. That does not frighten me. What frighten me are the facts of my 32 years, the years thrown away on medicine, and my illness and weakness. I have a stupid tumour behind my ear, which has been operated on twice. I am afraid that blind illness will cut short my work. If it does not, I shall do better than *Psalm*. Now I shall study to learn. The voice that disturbs me has to be prophetic. It has to be. I can become nothing other than one thing: a writer. So let us wait and see, and learn, and keep silent.

1924

8 January

Today the papers are carrying a bulletin on the health of Trotsky. It begins: 'Leo Trotsky fell ill on 5 November last year ...' and ends: 'He has been given leave and has been completely freed of all responsibilities for a period of not less than two months.' This historical bulletin needs no commentary. And so on 8 January 1924 Trotsky has been removed from power. What will happen to Russia, Lord alone knows. May He help her!

This evening at Boris's. My wife and I have just returned. We enjoyed ourselves. I drank wine, and my heart is not sore. The chervonets [unit of currency, backed by gold, introduced in 1922] is now worth 36 thousand million roubles ...

22 January

Just now (5.30pm) Semka told me that Lenin has died. He says there's an official announcement.

25 February. Monday.

This evening I received from Petr Nikanorovich the latest issue of [the almanac] *Nedra* [The Depths]. It contains my story *Diavoliada* [Diaboliad]. This was during my reading – I was reading extracts from [the novel] *The White Guard* at Vera Oskarovna's. It seems to have made an impression in this circle too. VO has asked me back to continue with it. And so I have been published for the first time not on the pages of a newspaper and not in a slim journal but in an almanac volume. Yes indeed. How much torment it costs! Notes on Shirt-Cuffs are dead and buried.

15 April. Tuesday.

Many people with 'good surnames' have been arrested in Moscow. People are being exiled again. DK was here today. As usual he is full of fantastic rumours. According to him, there is a manifesto circulating in Moscow released by [the Grand Duke] Nikolay Nikolayevich. Devil take all the Romanovs! They're all we need!

There's a campaign to re-run the elections for the management of house associations (to throw out the bourgeois, replace them with workers). The only house where this is impossible is ours. With not a single bourgeois on the management there's no one to replace. ❏

©Mikhail Bulgakov
41(1): 173/177
DOI: 10.1177/0306422012438663
www.indexoncensorship.org

This diary extract first appeared in *Index on Censorship*, August/September 1991, Vol 20 No 8

DATA NOW

Ana Arana

When the headless corpses of a young couple were found in a burning car in one of Mexico City's most exclusive shopping malls, the story made the front pages. If the bodies had been abandoned in a low-income neighborhood, as has been the trend, the news would have only been published as a small sidebar in a much less prominent position.

Mexico today is one of the most dangerous countries for journalists. As drug-related violence spreads throughout the country, reporters continue to work under extreme circumstances. Since 2000, more than 70 journalists have been killed in attacks carried out by organised criminal gangs battling over drug routes to the United States amidst a growing international drug market. Most of the threats affect the provincial media; in comparison, the national press based in Mexico City has faced few security problems.

In 2010, an investigatión conducted by Fundación de Periodismo de Investigación (MEPI) discovered that the regional press recoiled from reporting on violence in much of the country because of fear of reprisals. In 2010, newspapers published only three out of 10 stories about organised crime. But in 2011 there was a surprising turnaround. A MEPI report revealed that the regional press began bouncing back, with crime reporting largely restored, even in very violent cities such as Veracruz.

At MEPI, we monitored daily newspapers in 16 states, representing 65 per cent of the country, and found the change in reporting practices to be remarkable. The number of stories reporting on crime increased around the country. There were exceptions: in states like Tamaulipas in eastern Mexico, the press has been gripped by self-censorship after two criminal groups repeatedly harassed and threatened reporters, bloggers and those using social media to report on and spread information about criminal activity.

Editors at many local dailies have confessed that they do not publish the names of perpetrators or any specific details about individual criminal groups operating in their regions. It seems the print media has found a way to protect itself – by publishing articles that omit detail or thorough analysis and by not crediting individual reporters for content. In Sinaloa, Javier Valdez, founder of the independent weekly *Rio Doce*, says: 'One has to think about the narco when one writes a story,' adding that *Rio Doce* often publishes on criminal activity without going into too much depth.

The problem with reporting on violence without context or analysis is that this kind of journalism fails to equip readers with tools to understand their reality. Citizens may well know details pertaining to organised crime in small cities, but professional journalists are still needed to quantify the threat and look beyond anecdotal versions of events. In larger cities, a journalist can join the dots, make connections and explain why certain events occur – without this analysis, the population is at a loss.

Given the violence that journalists face in much of Mexico, there is a real need for data journalism – reporting that seeks to quantify events and make real, numerical sense of human suffering and significant events. Today's citizens need journalists to make social problems visible by turning complicated information into comprehensive news articles, graphs, timelines and maps. Yet in Mexico, and in much of Latin America, journalism still relies on anecdotal reporting that focuses on the individual testimonies of victims. In international journalism, when explaining why something does or doesn't work, evidence – statistics, detailed information and solid, multi-disciplinary research – is needed, in addition to strong and moving individual stories. As with current trends in journalism in the United States and Europe, journalists in Mexico must be equipped with the appropriate technology and employ methodologies used by other disciplines to make this possible.

In order to promote transparency and expose corruption, crime and social inequalities safely, there is a significant need for data journalism to be a part of the Mexican media landscape. Journalists' ability to go beyond anecdotal evidence and begin presenting the facts will not only help societies heal, it will help them understand problems and find solutions. ❑

©Ana Arana
41(1): 178/179
DOI: 10.1177/0306422012440061
www.indexoncensorship.org

Ana Arana is the director of Fundación de Periodismo de Investigación (MEPI) in Mexico City and *Index*'s regional editor in Mexico

OUT OF
THE DARK

Ariel Dorfman introduces an exclusive extract from his new play on peace and democracy in the Middle East after trauma and dictatorship

In 1991, *Index* was the first to publish the draft of a play that had not yet been staged and was eventually to be called *Death and the Maiden*. It was a claustrophobic work, dealing with the dilemmas of a transition to democracy in a country that might be Chile, but stood in for so many other wounded lands across the globe whose citizens were trying to figure out how to emerge from the past without forgetting its lessons or its pain and what to do with the unrecognised, often unnameable, traumas that they had suffered. I enclosed the story in a beach house and circumscribed the time to less than 24 hours in the life of three opposing protagonists and personalities, a supposedly limited microcosmos that 'represented' a vaster world outside where many similar people were facing the same fears and uncertainties. Of course, plays are never 'about' something. They should not attempt – at least mine do not attempt – to send a message or decide beforehand what the solution is to the terrors that haunt the men and women in that fictional universe. Even so, any work of art will inevitably reflect in some way, obliquely or more directly, the larger political and cultural framework within which it was given birth. More so, if it happens to be, like mine, a play where the state is itself

Death and the Maiden, the Royal Court Theatre, London, 1991
Credit: Alistair Muir/Rex Features

an overwhelming force in the lives of the characters, where state policies of forgiveness and investigation and justice determine those lives: what is allowed remembrance, what is silenced, who gets away with torture and who suffers the consequences, who gets to decide the national narrative and who is left out of power.

So the country just beyond the boundaries of that beach house is always lurking there, invisible but pressing down upon those two men and that woman. Which is why, in the final scene of *Death and the Maiden*, I broke all three characters out of the confines of those walls (really, the confines of their own minds), made them reconnect with each other in the public space of a concert hall, forced the real audience in the real theatre to see in the twisted fate of Paulina and Gerardo and Roberto their own collective destiny. The conflict up till then may have been circumscribed to these three and that beach house, but what happens to these people afterwards will be determined by history, by their further existence in a real country with real spectators, real victims, real accomplices.

Ever since that final scene, I have been wondering how to tell a story of a transition to democracy and its pitfalls, a story that could make the leap into history, get the epic treatment such a theme deserved, spanning decades. Like my play *Widows* (adapted with Tony Kushner from my novel), except that instead of focusing on a remote mountain village and peasant women whose men have been abducted, it would have at its centre the owners of power, the presidents and generals and opposition leaders – and their lovers, wives, husbands, consorts, subordinates. A play that dealt with many of the issues I had explored in previous work (disappearances, torture, truth commissions, resistance, complicity) but did so from the perspective of the rulers (I had dabbled with such a possibility in my play *Reader*, where the protagonist is a censor; but he was a functionary and not really in charge).

In a first version of that epic play, that I called *In the Dark*, commissioned by the Royal Shakespeare Company, I placed the action, almost automatically, in my home continent of Latin America – and indeed my play in Spanish, called *Desde la Oscuridad*, keeps that original location. But last year, as the Arab spring exploded and developed, I realised that to locate this story in an invented land in North Africa or the Middle East was to give it the urgency and immediacy and relevance it demanded. Of course, just as *Death and the Maiden* transpires in a simulacrum of Chile but was understood to be addressing a planet suffering through so many other parallel transitions to democracy, from Russia to South Africa, from East Germany to South Korea, so *Out of the Dark* also has shades of many other latitudes and longitudes, pain and secrets.

And because this is only an excerpt, only part of the first act, readers of *Index* won't fully know what those secrets might be, what hidden pain is yet to be revealed.

I hope that those readers will be able, in the near future, to find out the destiny awaiting the characters as the play continues towards its inexorable and, one would pray, redemptive end. Over 20 years ago, those who read *Index* back then, in 1991, had a preview of the play that would become *Death and the Maiden*. May *Out of the Dark* also take that journey from print to stage, from my feverish mind to the larger mind of our times, from the pages of *Index* into the world.

The time is now but covers a span of 20 years. The place is Tigris, an invented country in the Middle East or Northern Africa.

CROWD   Walid! Walid! Walid!

Lights rise on a crowd of men and women cheering WALID, a charismatic young Captain who appears in a spotlight, surrounded by soldiers. Behind him is another officer, in full uniform, KHALEEL. Walid salutes the crowd and they renew their chant in a frenzy.

WALID   ... a new dawn for our country, a new dawn for every last citizen of this land too long divided against itself. Not mere words, not false promises. The Movement of Captains has reached an historic agreement with our adversaries. Ali Mukhtar, leader of the Resistance ...

ALI MUKHTAR, a sombre man in his late 40s, appears behind. Walid and the crowd go wild again.
WALID   Ali Mukhtar and his men have deposed their arms and are ready to join our government. Not mere words, not false promises. My first decree as new president has been to free political prisoners, every last one.

The crowd cheers, and then a new chant begins.

CROWD   Jadiya! Jadiya! Jadiya!

WALID   Yes, Jadiya. At this very moment, a door to a cell is being opened, opened wide, and Jadiya, after five years in prison, is walking into the light, that unforgettable woman at last free. All of us walking with her, God willing, into the light of this new dawn, this blinding light of liberation.

A blackout.

In the darkness, we hear the sound of shovelling, leaves being scuffled, grunts. Lights come up on RABBIA, a woman in her late 40s, dressed in dark clothes. She is on her knees next to a mound of earth. She is carefully sweeping a site with a whisk. She sees something, snaps her fingers – and the FIRST ASSISTANT, dressed in a white doctor's gown, materialises out of the shadows, hands her a pair of pincers. Rabbia uses them to examine a bone. She deposits it in a cardboard box, then scrounges around in the mound of earth, finds what she is looking for: less than half a skull. She nods, hands it to the assistant, who puts it in the box. They cross the stage to a different space, where Leila waits in a chair. She is in her early 30s, dressed sombrely. Rabbia acknowledges her presence without stopping, continues on to an adjacent room only furnished with a table. As she puts on a white surgeon's gown and begins to assemble the remains on the table, the light fades on Leila.

RABBIA   Who is the murdered man? That's always the first question. Or is it a woman? Still the first question. Only later do we ask about the culprit. If indeed there is only one culprit. Can I have that –? Yes, thanks, that one. So. Where were we?

FIRST ASSISTANT   About the culprit?

RABBIA   You want to catch a killer. That's why everybody comes to work at the morgue. But at some point you'll realise no, we're here to serve the victims, listen to what their remains are still saying, doing God's work. Can you pass that? Even a splinter, that's all you'll need to detect, not much more, at times just a whisper of a hair, that's all, the remnants of a toe. And I can tell what berries this one ate – pincers, please –, if his father beat him. I'm his last friend. A ghoul, that's what I am. Does that make you nervous? That I'll eat him up?

2008 – Zimbabwe

Local and foreign journalists, along with members of the opposition, are attacked and arrested during the presidential elections in March. The violence follows the announcement that President Robert Mugabe's Zanu-PF party has lost its majority.

The SECOND ASSISTANT, female, also dressed in a white gown, enters breathlessly.

RABBIA   You're late, Nibras.

SECOND ASSISTANT   The soldiers stopped me, Doctor Rabbia. They told me he's coming here. Right now. The new president! Only an hour after he –

RABBIA   We have a crime to solve.

SECOND ASSISTANT   Doctor – the television –

RABBIA   Look at this forearm, can you see how it's cracked? Not by the teeth of a fox or a rodent, see – so –

FIRST ASSISTANT   A man?

RABBIA   Maybe he, maybe she – we'll find out, once we're into the rib cage –, ah yes, see how the fracture splits upward, as if she, maybe he, was trying to fend off a blow. Did they club you, my love? Was it with a stick? And here, in the quiet of this other bone, here's the answer. First a stick, then a knife.

Rabbia passes the bone to the first assistant, who drops it.

RABBIA   You want to work here? You'll treat each bone as if it belonged to your own mother, formed cell by cell inside a female body. It all starts, always, everything, with a female body. Guard this shiver of a bone as if it were the holiest of temples ...

First assistant leaves with the bone.

RABBIA   ... Until the day when we can repair more than one broken body, when the country is ready –

SECOND ASSISTANT   That's what they said on TV. That you've been chosen to head –

RABBIA   I don't believe in television. I believe in this femur.

Walid enters, with Khaleel and a soldier. Second assistant leaves.

RABBIA   Ah, and here he comes. You must be ...?

WALID   You don't recognise me?

RABBIA   You're the one who's been sending me messages, little messages, enigmatic, cryptic, for the last two years. Asking me if I'd be willing to serve, to help.

WALID   I didn't really expect a reply. But now –

RABBIA   You're in a hurry, of course, Captain Walid. Now that you're president, right? But ... no time for mourning, Captain President? Do we lose a mother, a father, everyday, now, do we? And here you are, their funeral just yesterday and here you are, in a rush, full of plans, pulsating with life, as if they hadn't died, as if your mother were still alive. Tell me why I should trust a man who recovers so quickly from the murder of his parents, from any murder, tell me that, Captain?

KHALEEL   The Captain President has not come here to discuss his feelings, Doctor. The country is in dire –

RABBIA   And you must be ... Captain. Khaleel, yes. Another one who sent me messages. Secret plans to redeem this land. Another one who has no time to mourn.

KHALEEL   In times like these, each of us has to put aside our own sorrows, our –

RABBIA   I met him once, you know, the Admiral. He came here, your father, just like you now, Captain Walid. Asked me to stay out of politics. Stay out of politics, he said, your father said, leave religion and politics to us, and we'll leave you alone, Rabbia, you can exhume all the bodies you want, you can console widows and comfort orphans, what do you say? And now, you have come to ask me to do the opposite. Here you are, the dead Admiral's son, eager for me to leap into politics, head his Commission – for Peace, right?

WALID   For Peace and Reconciliation.

RABBIA   Peace. Reconciliation. Names, names. When it's really about the bodies, eh, Captain? Bury them so they won't stink?

2009 – Philippines

At least 20 journalists are among those killed in the Ampatuan Massacre on 23 November 2009. A powerful clan with links to the government is accused of the attacks, widely recognised as the country's most devastating case of political violence.

WALID   I thought you'd be the first to want to put the dead to rest, Doctor.

RABBIA   Because nobody knows more about the dead than Rabbia, eh?

WALID   That, yes. But also: who has more integrity, more moral standing, is respected by all sides –

RABBIA   All sides in this conflict, yes, secularists against fundamentalists and traditionalists against socialists and mullahs against progressives, yes, all sides exalt me, the most renowned forensic doctor in the country, yes, distinguished even beyond our borders, and of ancient mountain heritage to top it all off – yes, yes, my fame – tales told by the press, publicity believed by the rabble. When what matters is that woman.

WALID   What woman?

RABBIA   Maybe you were in such a hurry you didn't see her out there, she faded into the wallpaper. But she's been coming to this morgue every morning for the last 12 years. And at the end of each day I go out and say to her – come and see what I say to her.

As lights rise on Leila, Rabbia goes to her. Walid, Khaleel and soldier follow but remain in the shadows.

RABBIA   Good morning, Leila.

LEILA   You have news, Doctor Rabbia?

RABBIA   No, my dear. There is still no news. Not about your husband. But that may change. Perhaps you should ask – we have a new president.

Walid steps forward into the light.

RABBIA   Perhaps you heard him on the radio, heard his speech. A new dawn for this country of ours, a new dawn for Tigris, right, Captain? Did you listen to him, Leila?

LEILA   As if my life depended on it.

RABBIA   He wants me to head a Commission. I'd have to establish the truth about the victims of the last 25 years of conflict. Anyone who lost a relative from one side or the other can come to this Commission and ask – what would you ask me, Leila, if I were to preside over it?

LEILA   I'd ask you to find my Bashir, track down the men who killed him, put his killers on trial.

RABBIA   I don't think that is what the Captain has in mind.

WALID   In effect, uh ...

LEILA   Leila.

WALID   We will find your husband's body, Leila. But my colleagues in the Armed Forces will only reveal information, his possible whereabouts, if they are guaranteed no retribution, no trials, no names.

LEILA No justice.

WALID As much justice as is possible, Leila. I will not lie to you. Neither the officers who have entrusted me with the presidency nor the guerrillas and religious leaders who have now joined our government of national unity are ready to have their past violence investigated. There is no democracy without a blanket amnesty for both sides.

LEILA   Somebody took my Bashir from our house that night. It was the night of our wedding, Captain. All I want is to look that person in the eye. Not jail, not for me to break his bones or burn his skin. Not revenge, Captain. All I want is to look at the man who killed him straight in the eye, slowly, up and down his body.

WALID   I can't offer you that. Only this: a chance for you and so many others to bury your dead, achieve some form of closure, make peace with God. The question is if Doctor Rabbia should join us in this effort. What do you think?

LEILA   I hope she says yes. Anything that brings my waiting to an end.

WALID   There is your answer, Doctor. The people have spoken.

RABBIA   But not Jadiya. What does the Mother of the Nation say to this plan of yours?

KHALEEL   Not a word yet, Doctor. Jadiya is being released from prison right now, as we speak. Who knows how she will react after five years in –

RABBIA   Who knows, who knows. That's the point. She knows.

WALID   You've met her?

RABBIA   Not even her shadow. I stayed out of politics, remember? But that's not what matters, is it, if I've talked to her, seen her shadow. Or her photo. What matters is if she trusts you. Because then you can count on people like me as well.

WALID   I'm about to meet her, in fact. In fact, she is probably waiting for me at this very moment, at the presidential palace.

RABBIA   Then this old witch should not keep you here. If Jadiya awaits your charms ... What will you say to her?

WALID   I will tell her the truth: that we need to bury the past, that we have to stop poisoning ourselves endlessly with the past!

RABBIA   Save your fiery words for her. You will need them, Captain President.

We hear the resounding thunder of a crowd chanting

CROWD   Who is our Mother? Jadiya! Jadiya! Jadiya!

Lights go down on Rabbia, Leila and Khaleel, as Walid crosses to an office in the presidential palace. Decorated with 19th-century furnishings. Portraits on the wall, a flag, a big desk with a stately chair behind it. Walid approaches the window, is about to look out, when Khaleel enters.

KHALEEL   She's here, Walid. Jadiya in person. And guess what? Still in her prison clothes. Said she wouldn't mind wearing them forever, if that's what it took to free the country from tyranny.

WALID   Good. As passionate as I've always imagined her.

2010 – International

WikiLeaks leaks 250,000 state department cables, embarrassing the United States and governments around the world. There are fears that the leaks may endanger a number of individuals.

KHALEEL   Passionate! Ready for some action, I'd say, after five years of abstinence. Maybe you can persuade her to take those prison clothes off, eh, Captain President?

WALID   That's not funny, Khaleel. I meant passionate for justice.

KHALEEL   How long do you intend to be President, Walid? Five years, 20, 30, how many?

WALID   As long as it takes to do the job.

KHALEEL   As long as you can get re-elected, you mean. Because we will be having elections now, Walid – and to win an election you'll need to pretend you have a sense of humour. So smile a bit more.

WALID I lost my mother and father a week ago –

KHALEEL   They were like parents to me too, you know how –

WALID   They're rotting in some hole, Khaleel, so don't ask me to smile at your jokes. I'm keeping my smile for Ali Mukhtar who is responsible for their death –

KHALEEL   We're not sure about that.

WALID   – and who I'm going to have to work with for who knows how long –

KHALEEL   He won't last, he'll resign, claim he represents the true Islam and denounce you as a secular devil, run against you in the next –

WALID   Even after he breaks with us, I'll have to smile at him, at his fanatical followers, smile at his sister who's out there with her prison clothes, but for God's sake don't ask me to smile at you. You're the one person I don't need to deceive about who I really am, how I really feel. Show her in.

Khaleel exits. After a pause, Jadiya enters. A woman in her early 40s, dressed in simple prison clothes. Alluring, seductive, restrained, majestic. They look at each other for a long while. Jadiya comes up to the desk, touches it. She crosses to the chair. She is about to sit in it, decides not to.

JADIYA   That's exactly where he used to stand, you know.

WALID   Your husband?

JADIYA   Exactly where you are now, General Walid.

WALID   I'll stay a Captain, thank you. Keeps me closer to the people. I think your husband would have approved.

She says nothing, keeps looking at him.

WALID   What was he like? What was President Mussa like?

JADIYA   President. I haven't heard anybody in the military calling Mussa that in – 25 years, since my husband was deposed, in fact.

WALID   Well, I'm calling him President. I'd liked to have met him.

JADIYA   Well, you might have, if your father –

WALID   I was hoping we wouldn't drag my –

JADIYA   – hadn't walked into this room, betrayed my husband. And I thought he was our friend, persuaded Mussa to appoint him Admiral, trusted him. *Where is Mussa, that coward?* The Admiral's first words to me. Because Mussa didn't stay here, wait to be paraded in a cage, in chains. *I'd rather they killed me.* And that's what they finally did, didn't they, didn't you? – killed him, dumped him in the ocean, scattered his remains in some field, some desert, you and your people, without even funeral rites.

WALID   I had nothing to do with –

JADIYA   So who was the coward? Who was the traitor? My man, victorious against the colonialists, elected by his people to be President? Or that other – man, your father, who crawled into this office and became the ruler of this land and used his guns to violently kidnap a woman six months pregnant with –

WALID   My father had many faults. And God knows I am going to correct as many of them as I possibly can. But nobody ever accused him of mistreating a woman –

JADIYA   Oh it was violent.

WALID   – and certainly not a woman who – I mean, my mother was pregnant at the time. I asked him once why he had allowed someone like you to be mistreated in –

JADIYA   Mistreated? Violently abducted, gagged, kept in a cellar for three months until my baby –

WALID   Jadiya, all your life you have been an advocate of dialogue, while your brother Ali Mukhtar preached jihad. *Only talking to each other can set us free.* Your words. Now. My father is dead and cannot defend himself. Please let me at least speak for him. Because my father always said that the men who dragged you to prison had disobeyed his orders. They hid it from him, told him you had left the country. Your loss was regrettable, he said, but –

JADIYA   Regrettable! I never even got to see my baby. They took my little girl away before I could even hold her in my arms, not even once. I awoke and she was gone. But you know what? She's dead. My little girl is dead, Captain. And there's nothing I can do to bring her back except to make sure no other mother, no other child ever has to go through something like that. That's why I'm here today, because I thought maybe this man is not like his father – and then I came into this room and I thought, yes, he is different. But I was wrong. This has been a waste of time.

She turns and starts to walk towards the door. Walid interposes himself, grabs her by the shoulders gently. She tries to break loose and cannot.

JADIYA   Just like your father. He also grabbed me. And now you'll tell me you're going to save the country, tell me, just like he did, *give me a chance, we both want the best for our country, we all want progress.* He was so close I could smell the breakfast in his mouth. Like now.

She sniffs him.

JADIYA   You even use your father's damn toothpaste.

Walid lets her go.

WALID   Do you know how long I've waited to meet you? No, hear me out. Because I've been listening to you, scrutinising your words. It's what an intelligence officer does. Gets to know the enemy. Think like the enemy, get into his skin, under her skin, get inside her, see the world from her eyes – and I did. I became a specialist in you. Hearing from you, about you, from every man, every woman I interrogated –

ADIYA   So you also interrogated women, you –

WALID   Hear me out! *Go to the huts, to the huts and fields and mines and factories, go there, to the origins, where the real people drag themselves through the endless mud of their days and nights. Touch their lives,* you said, *touch the lost children,* the prisoners said that you said, *be there when the baby dies from the lack of a vaccine, when the mother is beyond consolation, when there is one job for two thousand men and the husband gets drugged and lifts his fist to punish the wrong person, the woman close by. Ask yourself if we can afford to waste all those lives, if that can be what God desires.* No, no, hear me out. Because I went, guided by that voice of yours I had only heard on the clandestine radio when I was a child – right here in this room, as I played with my toys, my Dad and I listening to you after prayers, oh yes, he listened to you, and then later, by myself, surreptitiously, as I grew up, whispering to me, *tell me what would happen if we stopped plundering one another and started dreaming one another, tell me, tell me.* And now I can tell you, face to face. I listened, I learned. Like a child in school, like a child at his mother's knee. I am saying this to you, confessing this to you, this man who has just lost his own mother, what I could never have told my real mother.

Walid takes Jadiya's hand. She withdraws hers.

WALID   The fate of our country is in your hands, Jadiya. The people out there, they need something to give them hope, someone to lead them out of the darkness. Our two families have been feuding for 25 years. My father against your husband, your brother against my father, now me against you. Split on every issue, disputing who is really doing the will of God, ready to kill the adversary if he doesn't agree. But the riddle always stays the same. How to repair the past so it doesn't devour us? How to modernise this country and end the curse of hundreds of years of underdevelopment? How to leave the childhood of this country behind and stop crawling and start walking on our own two legs? How to be true to our religion but not shackled by it? Only one way, Jadiya. Repair the future, create a future where we act responsibly, seek accords, where such crimes, such fights to the death between brothers, race against race, rich against poor, one sect against another, are no longer conceivable. That's why

2011 – Middle East

Protests calling for democratic change spread across the region, beginning in Tunisia in December 2010. The Arab spring in Egypt, Libya, Syria and Bahrain leads to the resignation of more than one authoritarian leader.

you came here, why you'll help me. Because we can't always end up in the same place, impoverished and lost in this remote backland ...

JADIYA   ... impoverished and lost in this remote backland surrounded by deserts, yes, as if history had passed us by, as if history hated us, we who were once a great nation.

WALID   (*overlapping with her last words*) – as if history had passed us by, as if history hated us, we who were once a great nation, your words, your very own words. And I say, echoing you: we have to stop killing each other. We have to join forces.

JADIYA   You have my brother, Ali Mukhtar.

WALID   He's too ambitious, agreed to our terms much too quickly. Was ready to change clothes, let's say. And will change his clothes again, some-day, when it serves his purpose, helps him install an Islamic Republic. Whereas you ...

JADIYA   I have my prison clothes on. And if I –

WALID   If the woman who has been most damaged, who lost her baby and her husband, if she refuses to demand anything from that Commission that starts its work tomorrow – just like me. I will not track down the men who murdered my parents. If you join me and don't appear in front of that Commission, that sends a message, allows the citizens of this country to believe that it's possible to turn the page, start anew ... Is that too much to ask of you? What I'm asking of myself?

Jadiya goes to the chair behind the desk and sits there.

JADIYA   This was his chair. Mussa used to sit here. Hazard a guess, Captain. Tell me how often I saw my husband in the last 25 years? Once. I saw him once in the last 25 years. Once. When I was released that first time, after giving birth, I came to the attic where he was hiding, came to him without the baby. Asked Mussa to forgive me for ... 'I didn't want it anyway,' that's what he said. 'That daughter would only have been one more person they could hurt, that they would be hunting down to get to me.' That's what he said. 'I couldn't have loved her anyway,' he said, 'because if they came and paraded her in front of me, I had to be able to tell those military bastards: kill her, cripple her, pierce her feet, throw her over a cliff, go ahead. You won't change my devotion to the people, to the cause.' Always talking as if he were

addressing a multitude. I never saw him again after our meeting in that attic 25 years ago. 'I don't want to be tied down by you, by anybody. And I don't want you to know where I am, identify me, if they come for you.' As if I could have recognised him anyway. Mussa. The master of a thousand disguises, the man with a thousand faces. Just now you confessed what you've told no one, not even your mother. Here's my truth, Captain Walid: after a while, I didn't want him to come back to me anymore. Oh I loved him, like you love a ghost, like you love a song nobody sings anymore. Messages would arrive from time to time. The last one – five years ago, just before I was arrested myself a second time, and then ... nothing. They must have picked him up and ... You know what, Captain? It won't be that hard, what you're asking of me. I wouldn't have done it anyway, humiliate myself in public, crying about that stranger who was my husband, crying about him in front of some old crone on some Commission. He's dead, Captain. He died a long time ago. But my daughter. She still hurts. That I never even got to see her face.

WALID   Someone has to have accorded her a burial. We could –

JADIYA   I don't want to know.

She holds back her tears, manages not to break down. Walid watches for an instant, then embraces her.

WALID   I understand, I –

She breaks away.

JADIYA   Nobody understands. I could have saved her. If I had left with her father, but I was so arrogant, so sure of myself, *you go, Mussa, I'll be fine, I know how to defend myself,* and then I spat those insults out to your father and – oh my poor baby. Maybe she would have died anyway, was fated to die, would have been born ill in the best hospital in the world – but I keep thinking that if her birth hadn't been in that hellhole, she'd be alive today if I hadn't – if her mother hadn't been ... me.

Walid touches her shoulder. She takes his hand away.

JADIYA   And now, I'm lost, Walid. Who will save me from my ghosts? Or do you have some sort of magical formula which would return me to the times when we lived in peace in this land?

WALID   If you decided to join me ...

JADIYA   You're not as smart as I thought you were, young man. Your mother – oh, I once loved her dearly – was much more cunning. If she were here, she'd tell you to wake up, realise that I've already said yes, that you can count on me. And I'd hoped you had inherited some of her brains. But I'll be nearby to make sure you make no mistakes. So – you want me to announce that we've reached an agreement, let's say 20 years for the Commission to investigate, is that a good compromise, will that satisfy you?

WALID   There's only one thing that will satisfy me now, Jadiya.

She turns her back. Walid puts his hand on her neck.

JADIYA   I don't think this is a good idea.

She does not reject him. Walid embraces her from behind.

JADIYA   My husband wouldn't – he wouldn't like this sort of –

WALID   He's dead. You said so.

JADIYA   Yes.

He kisses her neck.

JADIYA   No. Not that.

WALID   You've been waiting for me to do this since you walked through that door.

JADIYA   You know that much about women?

WALID   I don't know anything about women. But you – it's as if I've known you all my life.

JADIYA   Things men say to women. My husband said exactly that all those years back, the first time he invited me into this room. Word for word.

WALID   And did it work?

JADIYA   Yes. But this is different. I was 17.

WALID   Yes. I'm the young one now. I'm the one who needs to learn.

He kisses her. She hesitates and then responds. Lights fade. We hear Jadiya's voice as a spotlight rises on Rabbia, alone, by herself, listening to the radio. Jadiya is interrupted often by cheers.

JADIYA   ... why we support this Commission for Peace and Reconciliation, this moderate revolution. This is our pledge. We will honour the dead, bury the dead. But, God knows, we will not be chained to the dead.

Rabbia nods, switches off the radio, lights fade on her, rise on Safeer and Hannah, bathed in the light of a television screen, a cradle nearby. We see Jadiya, sumptuously dressed, delivering her speech. Behind her are Walid and Ali Mukhtar. A crowd surrounds them.

JADIYA   The time has come for the fisherman to go out and catch fish at dawn. Fish, not bodies. He's tired of dragging up bodies with his nets. Just as our soldiers are tired of the endless ocean of killing.

A baby cries in the home. Hannah comforts the child, rocks it in her arms, continues watching the speech.

JADIYA   I am sure all the citizens realise what it means, that my brother and I should be part of this process of national unity, that we are ready, as our Captain President is, to turn the page, dream a land without retribution and recrimination, a land where tomorrow matters more than yesterday, where everybody can worship God in their own way without fear.

Cheers from the crowd. Ali Mukhtar steps forward.

SAFEER   Look, look, Hannah, it's Ali Mukhtar. It's really him. God, when I think how we searched for him.

HANNAH   Well, it's good you didn't find him. Listen!

ALI MUKHTAR   Fellow citizens: like my sister Jadiya, I believe in a land free of misery. But the Resistance has not forgotten why it was born. I am part of this government in order to guarantee that our righteous programme, the goals of our dead martyr, our great President Mussa, the plan of God, will be achieved. I do not sleep. Long live Tigris!

More cheers, as lights fade on Jadiya, Walid, Ali Mukhtar and the crowd. Safeer clicks off the television set.

HANNAH   So. Are you going before the Commission? Speak to them? You must know something, have seen something. Somebody threw my father down those stairs, maimed him for life, somebody must know –

SAFEER   Not this, Hannah, not again. We settled this! My hands are clean, what could these eyes of a lowly Sergeant have seen? I swore to you, on my knees, that I'd resign from the military if that's what you needed, and I did, woman, gave it all up for you, we made love right here, made our Alma right here, on this couch, what more do you want?

HANNAH I want you to say it again.

The baby starts crying.

SAFEER   I swear it by – by our little girl. I saw nothing, did nothing.

HANNAH   You swear it by our Alma?

She passes him the baby.

SAFEER   As God is my witness.

©Ariel Dorfman
41(1): 180/199
DOI: 10.1177/0306422012438651
www.indexoncensorship.org

NECESSARY DANGER

Veran Matic

In 1999 and 2000, after being banned for the fourth time by Milosevic's regime, B92 continued to broadcast online and via transmitters throughout Serbia. I was arrested, but after my release I was given 24-hour police protection, so the police were familiar with every step I took.

Some ten years after democratic change in Serbia, at least four journalists live under 24-hour police protection due to continued death threats from organised criminal groups. My colleague Brankica Stankovic was given 24-hour police protection, and a year ago, it happened to me too. The police believe our lives are in danger, but their protection now has the same effect as it did in the late 1990s and early 2000s – that of intimidation.

Colleagues from other media outlets are also under surveillance, but B92 faces specific threats against the way we work, against our determination to serve the public interest without compromise, to not give in to criminals, drug dealers, business tycoons and politicians. The threats are an obvious and direct attempt to silence investigative journalism in Serbia.

Following B92 broadcasts exposing organised crime and illegal activity, people were sent to jail and some big businesses had moratoriums placed on them or went under. But we never imagined that we would at any point need protection. We still don't understand it. We have lost our privacy; our ability to move about freely is hampered. We live with the psychological effect of not being able to make a move without a bodyguard – a feeling of agitation rather than one of being comforted. But it's very important that we don't let it depress us.

We at B92 were given a clear choice: to withdraw and wait for those who threaten us to be arrested, or to keep fighting. We decided to fight more fiercely, increasing the number of people working in investigative journalism and training new journalists. This refusal to withdraw has not helped ward off those who threaten our lives – but we must show our dedication to the standards of our profession and keep working.

Because we have worked through several wars and under bans, we recognise the signs of danger. We check out information about threats, even if it comes from friends, so that we don't become paranoid and make bad judgments. This takes up time and energy, but it is certainly necessary in order to keep a grip on reality.

For years now, the profession has been compromised. There is a clear erosion of ethics. Newspapers are more expensive, not because of improved quality but because the cost of paper has increased. Media is measured by profit, not by the number of quality investigative stories published. Advertising agencies are more important than editors, who are judged by the number of papers sold and on their ability to bring in advertising.

I am unable to do anything except practise ethical journalism linked to the romantic values of public interest. At B92 we take corporate social responsibility seriously. In 2011 alone, we raised more than €2 million, providing vital equipment to children's and maternity hospitals, food to Serbs living in Kosovan enclaves and paying for the construction of safe houses for victims of domestic violence. Almost a fourth of our advertising revenues were spent on social responsibility. Some have argued that this is not our job. But I don't think it is enough to expose the problems.

Independent investigative journalism cannot survive if we do not find new models that will allow us to work without relying on the country's most powerful networks. These changes must take place not only in the financial sphere, but also in education, culture, social relations and value systems. The role of the media is crucial, from a political perspective, but also as a moral issue on which the development and prosperity of the whole community depends. An environment that lacks media credibility cannot cherish democracy and human rights. We must restore the reputation of the journalism profession. B92's efforts have been significant, but we also need the support of international institutions that recognise that the welfare of the world's people can only be realised through socially responsible media. ❏

©Veran Matic
41(1): 200/201
DOI: 10.1177/0306422012438822
www.indexoncensorship.org

Veran Matic is editor-in-chief and president of B92's board of directors

REUTERS/Arko Datt

TRUSTLAW

EMPOWERING PEOPLE THROUGH INFORMATION

Looking for high-impact pro bono opportunities in your country or elsewhere? Or free legal assistance?

Interested in the latest on women's rights and corruption worldwide?

TrustLaw is a free global service designed to make it simpler for lawyers to engage in pro bono work and easier for NGOs and social entrepreneurs to access free legal assistance.

TrustLaw is also a global hub of news and information on good governance, anti-corruption and women's rights from our correspondents and content partners. The site includes articles, blogs, case studies, multimedia and country profiles.

trust.org/trustlaw

THOMSON REUTERS FOUNDATION

THELONGVIEW

How high is the price of hate speech, asks **Ursula Owen**, and who pays?

It was in 1993, four years after the fall of the Berlin Wall and two years after the official end of communism, that I became editor and chief executive of *Index on Censorship*. By that time it was becoming clear that the void left by the fall of communism was not, on the whole, being filled by parliamentary democracies or thriving economies. In the search for new social and economic imperatives in these new states, the temptation to assert identity by expressing intolerance of 'the Other', to turn to xenophobia and racism, was becoming a disturbing reality. Yugoslavia was breaking up, and by 1993 the Bosnian war, characterised by bitter fighting, genocide and ethnic cleansing, was in full flood.

When we relaunched the magazine in its new format in the spring of 1994, with Ronald Dworkin's seminal essay 'The New Map of Censorship' and Umberto Eco's 'Tolerance and the Intolerable', daily reports were confirming the rise of the New Right across Europe, and with it the rise of hate speech – that form of expression that is excluding, dehumanising, abusive, inciting to discrimination and violence. So the paradox of history was turning out to be that racism had increased as democracy spread through the post-communist world. Perhaps not such a paradox: as Hans Magnus Enzensberger once said: 'With democracy, all the dirt comes out.'

Hate speech, free speech absolutists say, is the painful price we must pay for safeguarding free expression above all other rights. But how high is the price and who exactly is paying it? Dworkin held the absolutist view. Free speech, he said, is what makes people feel human. Each citizen must have not just a vote but a voice, and by silencing people whose words we abhor, who pour race hatred into the culture in which we must all live, we forfeit the right to insist they obey democratic laws. Eco thought differently: we must define the limits of tolerance, he said, and must first know what is intolerable.

I drove through Croatia and Bosnia in 1996, just after the signing of the Dayton Peace Agreement which ended the Bosnian war, with eight busloads of journalists, lawyers, human rights activists from Europe, especially Serbia and the US. We were going to a conference in Tuzla, to support the social democrat mayor there in the post-war world. What we saw in the scorched landscape and shattered villages on our long journey through this beautiful country were the pathological effects of hate speech. Here the Others – people to be eliminated, slaughtered, driven away – were often well known to you: your neighbours, friends, even kin by marriage, made alien and terrifying by unreason perpetrated in the name of higher interests, under set slogans. The houses, streets and villages from which people were driven were not simply ruined by arson and looting; after the fighting they had been systematically crushed and destroyed with bulldozers and dynamite. So hate speech here had resulted in one of the ultimate forms of censorship – the obliteration of memory of a place, as if these lives and communities had never been.

I gave many talks in the mid-1990s on hate speech and in 1998 we devoted an issue of the magazine to the subject. I asked the question, as a dedicated opponent of censorship: if words can turn into bullets, is there a moment where the quantitative consequences of hate speech change qualitatively the argument about how we must deal with it? Is there ever a point of necessary intervention somewhere in the continuum between the ugly, offensive but more localised expression of hatred and the successful establishment in a community or society of a culture of hatred, where the instigators of hatred become the authorisers? And if so, how would it be done? And who decides? I got a lot of flak for writing this, and a lot of support. I was only asking a question. On one occasion I was talking to a group of free speech activists and novelists. At the end of the talk all the free speech activists said I was wrong even to ask the question; all the novelists said I was right. I'm still a passionate proponent of free speech, and I still think that hate speech, in its various manifestations, is the most difficult and tangled question we have to address. ❐

©Ursula Owen
41(1): 203/205
DOI: 10.1177/0306422012438657
www.indexoncensorship.org

Ursula Owen was chief executive and editor-in-chief of *Index on Censorship* from 1993–2006

Aftermath of the Balkans war, Sarajevo, Bosnia, 1996
Credit: Sipa Press/Rex Features

MANIFESTO

SPEECH CRIMES

Alexander Abdo

Americans cherish the right to free speech perhaps above all others. Uninhibited expression fuels our democracy, and it is conventional wisdom that an unregulated marketplace of ideas promotes sounder policy. And yet, in times of crisis, our government too often suppresses the right to free speech.

In the frenzied aftermath of 9/11, Congress passed, and President George Bush signed, the Patriot Act. Among other things, the Act expanded the laws criminalising the provision of 'material support' to 'foreign terrorist organisations'. The list of 'foreign terrorist organisations' is generated by the Secretary of State with virtually no meaningful oversight. And the government has interpreted 'material support' to encompass even speech intended to further peaceful and lawful alternatives to violent protest.

Last year, the Supreme Court upheld the government's sweeping interpretation of 'material support' in the *Holder v Humanitarian Law Project* case. In the case, humanitarian organisations proposed to advise several designated 'foreign terrorist organisations' – including the Kurdistan Workers' Party and the Liberation Tigers of Tamil Eelam – how to peacefully resolve disputes and to petition the United Nations for relief. In a divided opinion, the Court affirmed the government's authority to criminalise this speech.

In the years since 9/11, the government has not hesitated to prosecute pure speech as 'material support'. Tarek Mehanna, a resident of Massachusetts, was recently convicted of conspiring to provide such support by translating extremist videos and texts freely available online. Javed Iqbal pleaded guilty to providing 'material support' to Hezbollah by providing broadcasts from Hezbollah's television station (along with Christian channels and adult entertainment) to American customers. And Sami Omar al Hussayen was prosecuted for (although ultimately acquitted of) supporting terrorism by moderating an email group that discussed, among other things, violent jihad.

Not all threats to free speech are so direct. Since 9/11, the US government has developed the ability to monitor virtually all electronic communications of Americans and Congress has handed broad authority to the executive to use that ability to sweep up vast swaths of our international communications. The ability to dissent through confidential communications may very well be chilled by the government's latest surveillance efforts.

If there is reason to be hopeful, it comes from the oft-cited reflections of Justice William J Brennan, Jr on 'the shabby treatment civil liberties have received in the United States during times of war and perceived threats to its national security'. Justice Brennan noted the cyclical nature of the nation's response to traumatic events: after each crisis had abated, the country had 'remorsefully realised that the abrogation of civil liberties was unnecessary'. Though he hoped that these successive realisations would eventually fortify the collective conscience against such overreactions, he took some comfort in the apparent inevitability of national self-correction.

Can we be so sure that we will self-correct this time? A decade on from the crisis that drove politicians to once again stifle unpopular speech (albeit in the quest to prevent unlawful conduct), fear still pervades our politics. And unlike past overreactions, where the targets of our policies were our neighbours, the modern-day victims of our overreaching policies are largely faceless and voiceless in the national debate.

Still, there is reason for hope. In a series of cases challenging the worst abuses of the post-9/11 era, a handful of jurists have signalled a willingness to question, rather than defer to, the claim to a national-security override to civil liberties. Some politicians have suggested a desire to reassess the United States's war footing in light of the apparent hobbling of al Qaeda's leadership. There is hope, perhaps, that these doubts will mature into the self-correction predicted by Justice Brennan, and that the speech restrictions following 9/11 will be viewed as the latest Sedition Act. To achieve that goal, however, Americans will have to join these courageous voices of dissent and demand that our leaders respond to the challenges of national security with the recognition – demonstrated time and again – that our values are the very foundation of our strength and safety. ❐

©Alexander Abdo
41(1): 206/207
DOI: 10.1177/0306422012439503
www.indexoncensorship.org

Alexander Abdo is a staff attorney on the ACLU's National Security Project

INDEX
ON CENSORSHIP

INDEX ON CENSORSHIP 2 1999

BLAIR'S LABYRINTH

Tony Geraghty's book on Northern Ireland led to a police raid and his arrest: a chilling taste of brave new Britain

More than 20 years ago I was discussing political manipulation, censorship and sexuality with the novelist James Baldwin. Baldwin – former Harlem preacher and *New York Times* reporter covering the first of Martin Luther King's marches – wore a fetching caftan. He was attended by acolytes, living as a left-handed, homosexual, black American, socialist exile in Provence. He intoned, in Bible-reading rhythms: 'Listen! If they got you watchin' that thing danglin' 'tween your legs, they don't need no CIA to watch you. And why is that you ask? Because you – You! – is watchin' yourself!' His cascading laughter was a shrill, mocking message that no words of mine could capture.

I have thought much of that conversation lately, since 6.50am on 3 December to be precise: the moment when six detectives from the Ministry of Defence Police knocked on the door of my 17th-century cottage, in reassuring, rustic Herefordshire, and arrested me.

Censorship, I was about to learn, was more than a concept of abstract concern to – as Alastair Campbell would put it – 'middle class wankers'. It is a physical and psychological experience that leaves the victim feeling that he has contracted a political version of Aids, a sense that his privacy was illusory; an awareness that nothing committed to paper or computer or spoken within earshot of a microphone, in or out of the police interrogation room, is safe. The surveillance apparatus of the state marks home and hearth with an odour of fascism that no amount of liberal discussion can deodorise or exorcise. What is lost is the sense of self-possession itself, the very belief in freedom.

Was my name Geraghty? Had I written a book entitled *The Irish War*? Yes and yes again. I am a recidivist among writers, at it as journalist and author since I left

British soldiers on the streets of Londonderry, Northern Ireland, 1971
Credit: Bruno Barbey/Magnum

school, aged 16, on 18 December 1948. The eerily polite MoD team, five men and one athletic woman to keep an eye on my even more athletic wife, spent the next seven hours and 30 minutes searching a home crammed with files and books. At about 2.30pm they left with my computer, modem, many files ... and myself, in an unmarked car. It was not unlike a day in Nigeria in 1968, during the Biafran War, when four other polite men, their ritual scars identifying them as Yoruba, put me into an anonymous Mini for a long drive to captivity in Lagos. The only difference, this time, was that I, the prisoner, had to direct my captors to the local police station. There, the local station sergeant had trouble choosing the appropriate computer heading for my case. 'We don't get many official secrets cases in Leominster,' he explained.

I spent the next five hours in custody for two sessions of questioning about pages in my book describing how computerised surveillance systems, necessarily evolved for an exotic war across the water, are now being deployed against civilians in mainland Britain. In particular, the MoD men wanted to know about my sources and were clearly irritated when I spoke about the 'sanctity' of such things, even when they are gift-wrapped by the Downing Street lobby system. Another, similar session followed on 29 January, at which point the matter was passed to the Crown Prosecution Service. The CPS, advised by the attorney general, will have to decide whether I am to be the first writer to be prosecuted under Section 5 of the Official Secrets Act 1989, that part of the censorship law specifically aimed at scribes. The maximum sentence, on conviction, is two years.

In view of the release rate of convicted terrorist murderers and other political psychopaths, I doubt whether I shall have the chance to compare notes with any of them if I go down later this year. Meanwhile my book, the source of the trouble, a hypothetical threat to national security, continues to be sold freely throughout the realm.

Whatever the outcome I am surprised, as a battle-hardened old fossil, to be scarred by the censorship experience so far. Before the raid I had had intimations that something nasty was about to happen but I disregarded most of them, not wishing to surrender to paranoia. This, after all, was Britain 1998, not 1940, not Britain with her back to the wall, the blitzed London of my childhood, and with that, the experience of being buried under a building demolished by a flying bomb. This was also Blair's Brave New Britain. As for those Irish Republicans and their families, well of course they were asking for it. I had even made a neat, cerebral comparison in my book between the crude resettlement of hundreds of thousands of civilians into fortified villages in Malaya, necessary to win that war 40 years ago, with its modern equivalent: a selective, invisible, electronic cage that is thrown around neighbourhoods, families and individuals, thanks to systems with such engaging code-names as 'Glutton'. But this was not the stuff of real life in the hamlet of Hope-Under-Dinmore where I had chosen to put down some roots, at last. Or so I thought.

The raid went through the dirty linen basket and the erotica, some of it collected for a novel which links themes from ancient mythology – bestiality and incest – with modern practice. The team were careful and systematic. One did the scale drawings, showing the layout of each room as it was searched. Another, donnish figure claimed to be the computer expert. Two more went for the documentary evidence. A fifth man – sweating unnaturally most of the time – claimed he was the photographer but was clearly incapable of attaching a wide-angled lens to the camera with which he seemed strangely unfamiliar.

I was reminded of an account of infantry soldiers searching homes in Northern Ireland, dressed in their camouflaged 'cabbage suits', accompanied by a suitably disguised technician from MI5, whose job it was to plant the bugs. The subjects of that search, veterans by now, said to each soldier: 'Yuz are real "Angle Iron"' [Royal

Anglian Regiment] 'but you' – pointing accusingly at the odd man out – 'yuz is fucking MI5. Get out of here.'

The cost of an electronic sweep for hidden microphones – £1,200 – was more than I wished to pay at this point. Instead, my wife and I now take a walk whenever we wish to discuss sensitive issues; or sit in the bathroom with the taps running. We arrange for letters that we prefer are not exposed to government spies to be sent to a friend's address. Our neighbours, hearing of the raid, reacted like Frenchmen under Occupation and offered barns, outhouses and attics as places of further concealment, were that ever necessary.

About two days after the raid, a hazard warning light flashed on the steering wheel of my Peugeot, indicating an airbag fault. I drove to my local garage and asked the chief mechanic – an old soldier who knows the score – to check the vehicle for hidden devices. My telephone conversations are, inevitably, cryptic, and important discussions must now be face-to-face, far from any street.

Over-reaction? What is over-reaction? During my third interrogation session on 29 January it became apparent that the MoD Police (answerable to whom?) had accessed my credit card account for the preceding 13 months in order to determine on what day I had purchased a railway ticket for £27.05. The official effort invested in keeping watch on me was at a level appropriate to the sort of terrorist now being released from the Maze.

My real sin might have been to decline an invitation from a rear admiral in Whitehall, secretary of the censorship machine once known as the D-Notice Committee, to show him part of my book before it was published. The admiral, though on MoD's payroll, with an office in MoD Main Building, serving a committee chaired by the permanent under-secretary of that ministry, denies that he is answerable to MoD. In spite of that, I declined his invitation, since the censorship system that he runs, day to day, is notionally voluntary. Why was I so obstinate? After all, the vast majority of books on military affairs in this country is thoroughly censored, though the reader who buys them is never told that. (Should they carry a health warning?)

My experience does not instil confidence in their system. In 1992, the BBC Newsnight reporter Mark Urban submitted his revealing account of the undercover war in Ireland – Big Boys' Rules – for censorship, and he was betrayed. I know he was betrayed because an uncensored copy of the proof was passed to me in breach of the confidentiality Whitehall guarantees to those writers who collaborate with it. From the admiral's office, proofs are distributed to such agencies as MI5, ostensibly to be sanitised in the national interest. In practice, a mole-hunt begins to identify the author's sources. When the MoD's detectives came upon Urban's proof they asked: 'Has this been published?' I said it had. I had in mind the book, not the naughty bits. They put it back on the shelf and passed on. I now feel obliged to hide it a long way from home, just in case.

This is not quite a life on the run, but it has domestic parallels. I am now beginning – as James Baldwin said I would – to watch myself. Censorship is indeed a state of mind in which the mind is under siege. It is a process that occupies the sleeping as well as the waking state. It is a nightmare out of the pages of George Orwell and a labyrinth in which the victim encounters a minotaur partly of his own making. It is far from the Freedom of Information that Blair and his Lord Chancellor keep promising us. With luck, I might be in front of No 1 Court at the Old Bailey at about the same time as the next Queen's Speech. At least the enemy will then be tangible if no less real. ◻

©Tony Geraghty
41(1): 208/213
DOI: 10.1177/0306422012438320
www.indexoncensorship.org

Tony Geraghty is the author of *The Irish War* (HarperCollins, 1998). This article first appeared in *Index on Censorship* Volume 28, Number 2, March/April 1999

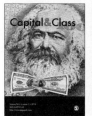  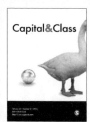
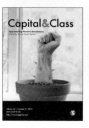  

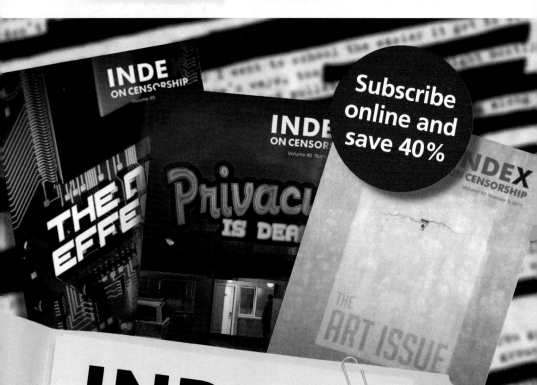